Keep
in
Memory

Keep in Memory

How to Enjoy Bible Memorizing

by

N. A. Woychuk, M. A., Th.D.

Executive Director
Scripture Memory Fellowship
Author, fifty-three memory books, "You Need to
Memorize Scripture," "Indestructible Nation,"
"The British Josiah," "Building Gold," "Servant of the
Living God," "Abide in Me"

Art illustrations by J. Emerson Russell, M.A., Th.M.

Foreword to Original Edition
Charles Lee Feinberg, Th.D., Ph.D.

Foreword to Current Edition by
Rev. L. Moffatt, B.S.., M.S.
Evangelist and Missionary

Scripture Memory Fellowship
P.O. Box 550232
Dallas, TX 75355
888.569.2560/scripturememory.com

9-0244

Keep in Memory
© 2006, Scripture Memory Fellowship

ISBN 1-880960-67-2

Cover by John Lautermilch

Printed in the United States of America

CONTENTS

Foreword to Original Edition

Yesterday, I took the day out to lay aside other things and complete the reading of Dr. N. A. Woychuk's manuscript on Bible memorization.

This is indeed a splendid piece of work. The English is a delight, and at times borders on the poetic. The abundant use of Scripture is most commendable, and the illustrations from actual participants over the years are unusually apt. I have read some of his writings before, but I find an added depth and dimension in this work. I have seen nothing like it in my reading through the years. I can only hope for a tremendously wide reading and application. I am convinced that it is a much needed and timely word for these days.

May 9, 1978   Charles Lee Feinberg, Th.D., Ph.D.
La Mirada,   Dean Emeritus
California   Professor of Semitics and Old Testament
             Talbot Theological Seminary

Foreword to Current Edition

This book is both timeless and timely. Some writings are seasonal, but this is an eternally up-to-date exposition of God's thoughts. We have known for years that God's Word is the cornerstone for our Christian walk.

The scripture found in Psalms 119:11 says, "I have hidden your word in my heart that I might not sin against you." This is a fact which we readily receive, but for some reason we do not totally get it done. When we get it done, we will be more fully aware of God's love that surpasses knowledge so that we may be filled to the measure of all the fullness of God.

This book spurs you on to get into the eternal message of God which is wonderful, but it has the added ingredient of telling why to do and how to do it. When you get into successful memorizing of scripture, your life takes on a totally new dimension and your ministry has a power it never had before and you are able to change lives and empower your personal ministry to a level you never thought possible.

This is a book that can continuously minister to you as you minister to someone who probably desperately needs to hear from God and you can be the capable and willing messenger of God's words of LIFE.

Rev. Robert L. Moffatt, B. S., M. S.
Evangelist and Missionary

March 27, 2006
Lee's Summit, Missouri

O Book Sublime!

If we could plunge to the depths of truth,
And grasp the whole rich story,
Our souls would rise to paradise,
Enraptured by its glory.

For boundless wealth lies in this Book
Resplendent as a treasure;
Its brilliant rays shine on our ways—
Availing without measure.

O Word divine; O Book sublime!
Oh wisdom so transcending!
We look to thee; we cling to thee
For guiding light unending.

—*Dr. S. Franklin Logsdon*

Chapter One

MEMORY

A little girl was once asked, "What is memory?" "Oh," she replied, "that's the thing that I forget with." And this may not be a bad definition because the right kind of memory *remembers to forget* certain things as well as *remembering to remember* other things.

The human mind is a masterpiece of God's workmanship, and with amazement each of us may well exclaim with the Psalmist, "I will praise thee: for I am fearfully and wonderfully made" (Ps. 139:14).

Advanced brain research is being conducted these days at an accelerated pace and is directed toward discovery of how the brain perceives, processes and stores information. Of equal fascination to the researchers is the persistence of memory, the ability not only to store but also to recall information and experiences. The brain switches emotions on and off; it responds instantly to the signals from the senses, but is itself not controlled by the senses. Unlike the computer, which can be turned off at the flip of a switch, the brain remains continuously active whether waking or sleeping. Like an image repeated a countless number of times in a hall of mirrors, the brain can think about itself as it thinks about itself thinking about itself!

Oliver Wendell Holmes said that "Memory is a crazy witch; she treasures bits of rags and straw, and throws her jewels out the window." Memory can be very fickle and remain capricious even after we have become new creatures in Christ Jesus. We seem to forget how God has lifted us up out of the miry clay and how He has led us all along the way. We forget His benefits (Ps. 103:2). We forget how we were "cleansed from our old sins" (2 Pet. 1:9). We forget or take for granted His mercy which endures forever. "Memory has some very big holes," a dear saint remarked, "and some big things drop away into oblivion." Our memories are defective, erratic and very unsanctified. Perhaps we fail to realize what a great trust God has given to each one of us when among many other endowments, He gave us the amazing capacities of the brain, including the one called *memory*.

God gave us memory, someone once said, so that we might have roses in December!

The memory is like a bank. The money deposited in a bank is not only safe, but it bears interest, yields dividends that accumulate with time. A mind stored with Scripture and other enlightening compositions is better than a large savings account. The precious promises of God will yield dividends, which, though intangible and imponderable, will be of more personal enrichment than material possessions. *William Lyon Phelps*, renowned literature professor at Yale for many years, used to encourage his students to substitute for answers to the examination questions, passages accurately remembered from *Shakespeare* or some other first-rate poet. He believed that it was better to know the writings of the distinguished authors by heart than it was "to devote themselves to problems of authorship, interpolations or textual criticism."

It is so much more profitable to have the enduring word of God itself in the memory than to be occupied with technical details in the study of the Bible or various theories and speculative interpretations which relate to it. Studying the Bible gets a person into the Word, memorizing it, gets the Word into the person.

And the rich dividends are inevitable as many will be quick to bear witness. *Mrs. G. H. Poppy* of Burnaby, British Columbia, said: "Ten consecutive years of memorizing the Word in your plans have been a rich blessing in my own heart and spiritual life. The verses are very valuable when I endeavor to share the joy of the Lord with others, but most precious as my personal source of strength, guidance, challenge and comfort . . . it has helped my children and me establish study habits that have enriched other areas of our lives as well."

And from Newberry, South Carolina, a young man, *Dan Young*, writes: "I am thankful for how God has blessed the memorization of Scripture in my life. The discipline has helped me learn the verses which have been encouragement, conviction, joy, growth, strength, true education, means of helping others, restoring me to fellowship and obedience, and showing me God's love."

The memory is like a garden! Flowers, fruits and vegetables come with care; weeds and thistles come with carelessness. A flower garden is supposed to fill the place with fragrance and beauty; an orchard is intended to produce fruit, not garbage. Let's face it. The excitement of lurid, romantic fiction, the rhythm and words of certain kinds of music do indeed appeal to the human nature. Immoral books, unclean pictures, suggestive stories fill the memory with "fleshy lusts," obscure the clear sky of the mind and dull the power of perception. But realizing it and talking about it is not enough. The Christian must study the Word diligently, memorize it exactly and follow it faithfully in order to be victorious. The evil must be supplanted with good.

Therefore, beginning with early childhood, plant the precious seed of divine truth and be assured of reaping a harvest of things that are pure and lovely and of good report. Plant in the "good ground" of the honest heart the "seed" of the Word and "it will bring forth fruit with patience" (Lu. 8:11-15).

"Be not deceived; God is not mocked; for whatever a man sows, that he will also reap. For he who sows to his flesh will of the flesh reap corruption, but he who sows to the Spirit shall reap life everlasting. And let us not be weary in well doing: for in due season we shall reap, if we faint not" (Gal. 6:7-9).

"We have matured in Christ since we have hid His Word in our hearts and it has taught us His ways," writes *Mrs. R. R. Hare*, Fort Worth. "It's so comforting and peace-giving to have God's Word hidden in our hearts" (*Mrs. J. Dunn*, Princeton, WV).

The memory is like the creative work of an artist. Self-conscious memory is the result of God's creative act. The artist transcends space and time and lives with absolute reality away from the body and away from the present. Through the exericise of his memory, past events assume reality and he puts on a blank canvas a vivid scene which he saw a thousand miles away and perhaps as many weeks ago.

This is how the Spirit of God uses the Word which we hold fast in memory (1 Cor. 15:2). "Has God forgotten to be gracious?" cries the afflicted one (Ps. 77:9). The reply rises in the heart that has meditated on God's ways and work (Ps. 77:12), "I will *remember*" — the memory is at work — "I will *remember* the years" and "the works of the Lord." "Surely I will *remember* Your wonders of old" (Ps. 77:10, 11), and most of all I will "*remember* Your love" (S. of S. 1:4). "Troubled . . . perplexed . . . persecuted . . . cast down" (2 Cor. 4: 8, 9), yet victorious in Christ through the simple God-appointed means of remembering the Word (Rom. 8:31; 1 Cor. 15:57). By believing, the troubled soul may live in a different world, above the disquieting circumstances, and almost detached from the body and the hopelessness of the present moment: "Yet the Lord will command His lovingkindness in the daytime, and in the night his song shall be with me" (Ps. 42:8). God's promises always carry a full guarantee: "You meet . . . those that *remember* You in Your ways" (Isa. 64:5).

Perhaps we have never really thought of dedicating our memory to God and taking care to fill it, not with man's words, however true and beautiful, but with the infinitely superior Word of God. "Wherefore, let us gird up the loins of our mind" (1 Pet. 1:13), redeem the time and more resolutely give ourselves to a disciplining system of Bible memorization. Memorizing is the best therapy for improving the memory; although I did recently read about "rosemary," which says an old writer, "It strengtheneth the memorie." Rosemary is an aromatic evergreen shrub in southern Europe which bears light blue flowers and is used in cooking and perfume manufacturing. Many years ago, there was the custom in certain parts of Europe to give every mourner at a funeral a spray of rosemary, which was taken home and planted in the garden—for remembrance.

There is many a rosemary planted in the garden of our hearts—lovingkindnesses of friends sent by the "Giver of every good and perfect gift": sometimes it is in the form of understanding words, or assurances of prayer; sometimes it's a visit of a loving friend; and then occassionally it is a special kind of gift. There's many a precious "rosemary" which each of us treasures. I can think of two very special ones right now: one is a hand with the forefinger pointing heavenward. It was painstakingly carved out of solid walnut by a dear brother, who like the Lord, "loves at all times." Another is an elephant about a foot tall, from Thailand. A very special note accompanied the carving: "This hand-carved teak-wood elephant from Thailand," wrote *Karen Pharnes*, from Mendon, Massachusetts, "is a small token of my appreciation to you for having a very large part in my training for His service. Without your vision given by Christ, there would be one less missionary nurse in Thailand. When you get discouraged, look at this elephant and *remember* all the Karens who have been trained for His service through your faithfulness."

Thank God for every friend who has planted a "rosemary" in the garden of our memory. Yes, thank God, for it is He who led us forth by the right way, so like one of old, we all may "Abundantly utter the memory of Your great goodness" (Ps. 145:7).

"My Rosemary brings
Of bygone things
A fragrance rare,
A sweetness where
There comes to me
Afresh to see
For every cross
And every loss
There has been more
From God's own store
Of joy untold
A hundred-fold."

No doubt all of us would like to be able to secure a large supply of what rosemary is supposed to do for us. The legend surrounding it implies that it helps you remember only the good things, and what we need possibly even more is some aid which would strengthen our "forgetterie"!

The Sanctification of the Memory

The full sanctification of the memory requires that we forget certain things:

1) *It would be a blessed thing if we could lose the remembrance of our injuries.* The sense of personal injury by other believers is aggravated by remembrance. "Wounded in the house of my friends" (Zech. 13:6) and "mine own familiar friend, in whom I trusted, which did eat my bread, hath lifted up his heel against me" (Ps. 41:9). This is a battle that, by the grace of God, we must win or it will consume our self-control, our gentleness, our meekness, and fill the chambers of our memory with bitterness and gloom.

2) *We must forget our forgotten sins.* There is the sin of yesterday which we have confessed, and which the gracious Lord has forgiven, and yet we turn to it again when the Lord Himself has buried it, and over its grave He has planted the lilies of peace. And if we should ever find ourselves in these fields of defeat, we ought to pluck and bring back with us a lily and testify to the glory of God that where sin abounded "grace

does much more abound." There ought to be no room in our memories for the heaviness and anguish of sin which has been completely forgiven by God and who declares: "I will *remember* their sin no more" . . . "I have blotted out, as a thick cloud, your transgressions" (Jer. 31:34; Isa. 44:22). Is not that enough positive instruction, dear friends, for us to do likewise?

3) *It would be profitable for us also if we did not retain in our memory past triumphs and attainments.* It is really true that some men's chains are found in their achievements. They linger over past days and gloat over their successes. When we thus sit down with our victories, progress and fruitfulness will cease. We must give earnest heed to the Apostle's strong and positive determination to forget "those things which are behind . . . and press toward the mark for the prize of the high calling of God in Christ Jesus" (Phil. 3:13, 14).

While we are often agitated and disturbed by not being able to remember certain things, we are all much more deeply troubled by not being able to forget! In *Joseph Conrad's* novel, *Almayer's Folly,* there is a most painful scene, where the daughter tells her father that she is leaving home forever, and that he will never see her again. She leaves the house, walks through the sand to the edge of the water, boards the ship and disappears from view. The anguished father, moving on his hands and knees, obliterates every trace of her footsteps in the sand, but he cannot take the trace of her little feet out of his heart!

4) *The grace of God is the only provision* for the sanctification of the memory. "Let this mind be in you which was also in Christ Jesus," who yielded His rights (Phil. 2:5-8), who reviled not again, who threatened not, "but committed Himself to Him that judges righteously" (1 Pet. 2:23). "Let this mind be in you," the Apostle insists. We must have a sanctified memory — God help us! It comes as a result of that direct, personal converse and communion with the Lord through a continual meditation on His word; it's that constant fellowship with God that gradually transforms the consciousness of the child of God. It is the blessed Holy Spirit who brings to remembrance the Word of the Lord and brings into view the reality of the living Person of the Lord Himself. It is by the fulness of His might that the spaces of our soul become dwelling places of eternal truth! Dear God, evermore, give us a hallowed memory that we may fervently pray as the saint of old, "Lord help us to *remember* what we ought not to forget, and to *forget* what we ought not to remember."

"Having Tasted Their Sweetness"

Queen Elizabeth I, of England, once said, "I walk many times in the pleasant fields of the Holy Scriptures, where I pick up the goodliest herbs of sentences, eat them by reading, digest them by musing, and lay them up at length in the high seat of memory by gathering them together; so that *having tasted their sweetness*, I may less perceive the bitterness of life."

Queen Elizabeth I, no doubt read and memorized from the *Geneva Bible* which was published in 1560, the year after her coronation, and which was dedicated to her out of appreciation for the fact that she favored the Protestant cause. Eight years after her death (1603), the King James translation became available.

Chapter Two

INSPIRATION . . . of the WORD

Some years ago, three freshmen students from the Tennessee Temple College, in Chattanooga, Tennessee, came by our booth at the Highland Park Baptist Missionary Conference; after examining the display for a little while, one of them said, "Have you developed any special techniques for memorizing?" "Yes, as a matter of fact we have," I said, as I sent up an urgent request, "Help me, O Lord." I thought on it a moment or two and said to them, "Yes, the Lord has given us some very practical techniques through the years for encouraging people to memorize Scripture. Here, may I quickly gather them up for you under five important words:

"(1) Assimilation
"(2) Concentration
"(3) Relaxation
"(4) Meditation
"(5) Application."

Of course, I elaborated on each one as I went along, and then encouraged them to enroll and memorize the Word of God in a systematic way.

You know, Bible memorizing is a vital subject and not much written information is to be found on it anywhere. Interested friends have prayed concerning this effort, and I trust that it will prove helpful to many. Now, instead of five significant words to guide us along in this endeavor, we have eleven.

The first is *Inspriation!* I trust that it will be a means of inspiring many to memorize the Scriptures and experience the special blessing that comes only as a result of committing the Word of God to memory. *Mrs. R. A. Campbell* of Crowley, Texas condenses the help of memorizing the Word, thus: "In elementary school it was truly my sword and stabilizer; and in high school my memory work helped

16

me in countless ways."

I am particularly hopeful that pastors and other Christian leaders in key positions in the churches, in the Christian schools and in other institutions will study this subject carefully so that they might be able to lead their people and make a big thing of it among their children, young people and adults. Let us adopt the principle, first of all, that reading God's word is good and essential, studying is better, but memorizing it is best of all. And although it is hoped that this effort will result in *inspiring and encouraging* many to have the Word of God written upon their hearts, the subject of this chapter deals basically with the *inspiration* of the Scriptures themselves.

Why should we memorize the ancient Scriptures? Because, this volume called the Bible, is the writing of God. It is the thinking of God. It is infinitely superior to everything that man has produced, including the most up-to-date philosophies and compositions. Each word in the Bible came from the lips of God. The framing of each sentence was controlled by the Holy Spirit. The Scriptures were initiated and formed in the mind of God, and then, by divine control, they passed into the minds of the Bible writers whom

17

God specifically prepared and chose to use in giving us His Word. Although human writers used their natural abilities, yet the things that they composed were distinctly set forth in Spirit-selected words, or as *Basil Manly* expressed it, "The whole Bible is truly God's Word written by men."

The Bible is a very unique book, yea, a miracle book, and it is quite exciting to think that we are actually reading and thinking upon that which has come to us from God in Heaven. It was very exciting to hear the voices from the moon when our astronauts landed there some years ago, even though we knew that those words were spoken by men who went there from our own planet.

Some time ago, there was much curiosity and real interest among scientists and astronomers regarding the possiblility of hearing some voices from Mars, which passed closer to Earth than it will do so again in a long, long time. They set up powerful radio equipment for the purpose of projecting reception from that planet. They listened expectantly all night long but not a sound was heard.

The Bible is not the word of men dwelling on earth; it is not a voice from moon-dwellers nor is it the word from the planet Mars. It is much more than that! It is the voice from Heaven. God has spoken! And when we memorize the Word of God, we are memorizing what God has said and what God wants us to know.

The Old Testament writers were confident that they were declaring God's truth. "Thus says the Lord" occurs more than two thousand times in the Old Testament. The New Testament writers most emphatically attested the divine inspiration of all Scriptures (2 Tim. 3:16; 1 Thess. 2:13). They recognized that Scriptures are the product of the creative breath of God. He uttered them. He breathed them out. Divine *inspiration* of the Scriptures covers not just "concepts" or thoughts, but it reaches to the very exact choice of the words used (1 Cor. 2:13), as well as to the subject matter. As *Bishop Westcott* observed, "Thoughts are wedded to words as necessarily as soul is to body." *Inspiration* then of necessity takes in both—the thoughts and the words. God said to Moses, "I will be with thy mouth, and teach thee what thou shalt say" (Ex. 4:12), and to Jeremiah He said, "I have put my words in your mouth (1:9), and to the prophet Hosea God said, "I have written to him the great things of my law" (8:12). The Scriptures are God's voice, not man's; the words are God's words, not man's. All the concepts and all the words in the Bible come from the eternal, almighty Creator, and they are forever "settled in heaven" (Ps. 119:89).

Long after the books on science, philosophy, history and other important subjects have passed out of existence, or paled into comparative insignificance, the blessed Book of God, the Bible, shall stand! It will stand because it is the "word of truth" (Jn. 17:17); it will stand because it is the "word of righteousness" (Heb. 5:13); it will stand because it is "the word of life" (Phil. 2:16). As we read and memorize the Scripture, it makes quite a difference when we remember that "it proceeds from the mouth of God" (Deut. 8:3) and as the Apostle Paul said, "Whatsoever things were written aforetime were written for our learning, that we through patience and comfort of the Scriptures might have hope" (Rom. 15:4).

"Concerning Thy testimonies," the Psalmist said, "I have known of old that Thou has founded them for ever" (Ps. 119:152). It is estimated that only one half of one percent of all the books published survive more than seven years. Error and falsehoods pass away, and the gems of man's wisdom soon fade and disappear, "but the Word of our God shall stand for ever" (Isa. 40:8). It abides because residing in it are some of the same qualities that characterize God Himself. It is incorruptible (1 Pet. 1:23); it is living, powerful, and discerning (Heb. 4:12).

Satan's strategy has always been to keep *unbelievers* away from the Bible or keep them from understanding it (Lk. 8:12), and to keep *believers* from assimilating its vital message which they profess to believe. "Keeping unbelievers away from the Bible can be accomplished in either of two ways," *Dr. Francis Steele* observes: "Shutting off access to the Scriptures by restrictions on publication or circulation of the Bible or by denying entry of missionary translators on the one hand or, shutting off interest in the Scriptures by undermining its authority or spreading lies about its message.

"Getting Christians away from the Bible," Dr. Steele continues, "is often being done most effectively simply by inducing them to *neglect* it. No matter how vehemently a Christian may claim to 'believe the Book from cover to cover,' if it is not used it is useless. Surely, this is the greatest problem in North America. Bibles are available everywhere in a variety of languages and translations and in many different price ranges.

"Sometimes the Scriptures are taken away from the Christians by force: in the early centuries Christians were consigned to death in the arena if they refused to hand over their Books; collecting Bibles and jailing Christians in the Middle Ages—and a number of countries today. . . . From the Garden of Eden to the end time, Satan's bitterest hatred, his strongest attack has been and will be upon the Word of God."

Satan and the whole world system is set against the Word of God and we see it manifested aggressively in the world's educational program, its entertainment, its philosophies and all its standards. Satan has vigorously battled the Word of God in every generation, including our own, when possibly more has been done to undermine the infallibility, the inerrancy and the verbal plenary inspiration of the Scriptures than in any other age. But in every generation there are the earnest-hearted believers who recognize that the Bible comes from God and that it speaks for God; it is this keen realization that makes them consumed with desire not only to assimilate the Word of God themselves but to see it implanted in the hearts of their children and all those for whom they feel responsible. In speaking about the "more sure word of prophecy" the

22

Apostle Peter said, "I think it is meet, as long as I am in this tabernacle, to stir you up by putting you in remembrance . . . moreover, I will endeavor that you may be able after my decease to have these things always in remembrance" (2 Pet. 1:13, 15).

The Bible is a wonderful book. It came to us from God, who moved men to set forth His thoughts in the Spirit's chosen words, "Wherefore you do well that you take heed," Peter said, "as unto a light that shines in a dark place, until the day dawn, and the day star arise in your hearts" (2 Pet. 1:19). The Bible is an eternal Book! Its message remains the same — unchanged and unchanging for every age and for every generation.

I visited the World's Fair in New York City in 1939. The *Time Capsule*, a huge torpedo-shaped shell made of Cupaloy, was buried 50 feet deep on Long Island at the World's Fair. It is to be exhumed 5,000 years later. More than 100 modern objects were enclosed in addition to microfilm and photos of contemporary life. It was proposed that the capsule is to be a means of acquainting civilization of the distant future with the achievements of our time. Except for the thin book of record explaining the capsule, only one full-size volume was enclosed. That was the Bible. An official of the company sponsoring the project was asked why the Bible was chosen. He replied, "The Holy Bible of all the books familiar to us today, will most likely survive through the ages. Therefore, the Bible that we place in the capsule will be a sort of connecting link between the past, present and future."

"Therefore, think not of it as a good book, or even as a better book, but lift it in heart, and mind and faith and love far, far above all, and ever regard it, not as the word of man, but as it is in truth, the Word of God; nay, more, as the living Word of the living God; supernatural in origin; eternal in duration; inexpressible in value; infinite in scope; divine in authorship; human in penmanship, regenerative in power; infallible in authority; universal in interest; personal in application and, as St. Paul declares, inspired in totality" (*Canon Hague*).

The Excellence of the Scriptures

"The Bible is a very unique book and all of it, from cover to cover, proceeds from the mouth of the Lord and is in all its parts equally inspired by the Spirit of God. However, there are certain portions which seem to speak to our hearts more directly and delight our souls with sacred joy. One such portion is Psalm 19. Read it through carefully, and as you read, consider its essential value compared to the writings of men.

(1) *The Praise of the Glory of God in Creation* (19:1-6). The "heavens," that is, the super-terrestrial spheres in infinite space, tell how great and how glorious is God! The "firmament," which is the vault of heaven spread out over the earth, proclaims the wonders He has wrought. The day tells of His power and beneficence; the night tells of His vastness, splendor, order and mystery.

They are "like the two parts of a choir, chanting forth alternately the praises of God" (*Horne*). Their message is inaudible and inarticulate but it is thoroughly intelligible to human beings throughout the whole earth. "The testimony of the heavens of God is understood by the peoples of every language and tongue" (*Calvin*). Their silent eloquence reaches every understanding heart, as *Addison's* interpretation points out:

"What though in solemn silence all
Move round the bright celestial ball?
What though no real voice nor sound
Amid their radiant orbs be found?
In reason's ear they all rejoice,
And utter forth a glorious voice,
For ever singing, as they shine,
'The hand that made us is divine.'"

The sun, chief witness to God's glory, is represented as a bridegroom full of joy, and as a runner full of strength. His beneficent influences of light and heat are universally felt. The morning sun sheds light whose freshness and cheerfulness is as the renewed energy and eagerness of youth. *Scroggie* refers to these witnesses as "celestial missionaries. . . . Sun, moon and stars are God's travelling preachers; they are apostles on their journey, confirming those who regard the Lord; and judges on circuit, condemning those who worship idols."

God has two great works of art! They are His *Poiema* — (from which we get our word poem). One speaks concerning the magnitude of His power — "things that are made" (Rom. 1:20) — and the other — "His workmanship" (Eph. 2:10) — attests to the magnificence of His love and mercy.

(2) *The Praise of the grace of God in His Word* (19:7-11). Suddenly, the Psalmist turns from the wonders of God's creation to the supreme perfections of God's quickening Word. The six effects of the Word which the covenant-keeping Jehovah has spoken are set forth in a striking manner: The "law," which tells of Divine instruction, restores the soul as food refreshes the body.

The "testimony" which attests to what God is, gives practical wisdom to those whose minds are open to the will of God.

The "statute," tells of man's obligations and brings delight to those who obey.

The "commandment," pure and authoritative as God is Himself, illuminates the darkness and brings understanding.

The "fear of the Lord," which speaks of the settled habit of the soul, unchangingly endures.

The "judgments" are all in accordance with the standard of absolute justice.

The Psalmist proceeds to evaluate the wonderful Word in a practical way: It is "more to be desired than . . . fine gold." *Scroggie* sums it up this way: "Gold is good, fine gold is better, much fine gold is best, yet God's Word is better than the best, and more to be desired." God's Word is better than honey and sweeter than the purest honey, which is the droppings of the honeycomb.

The word of God encourages, warns, restrains and for those who obey it and submit to it there is for them right now great reward — the reward of vision, the reward of power, the reward of manifold grace and the reward of enlargement of soul.

(3) *The Praise of the Goodness of God in His Forgiveness* (19:12-14). Contemplation of the Word inevitably leads to a quickened conscience: "But with all this affection for God's Word, there is mingled awe and reverence. That Word lays a man bare to himself. It judges him: it shows him what is in him, convinces him how much there is that needs to be purged, reveals to everyone how far he is from perfect obedience. It is at once a copy of the will of God, and a mirror of the heart of man. Hence it calls forth the penitent confession" (*Perowne*).—"Who can understand his errors? Cleanse thou me from secret faults."

This is followed by the earnest prayer that no sin—"secret" or "presumptuous" may gain the mastery over him.

In his evaluation of the Word, the Psalmist concludes: "Let the words of my mouth and the meditation of my heart be acceptable in your sight, O Lord my strength and my redeemer."

The heart meditates and the mouth utters it. How blessed it is and how pleasing it must be in the sight of God when the heart of the believer so meditates upon His Word so that when the mouth begins to speak it is articulating the very Word of God. Such meditation and such articulation, such praise and such prayer will always be acceptable in the sight of God and will fall like a heavenly benediction upon the ears of all who hear it.

Before proceeding with the reading of this book, how good it would be for each of us to memorize this 19th Psalm, or at least to shut off everything else, and read it, slowly, meditatively and, with deep earnestness, worship God for what He is and for the magnificence of His revelation:

The heavens declare the glory of God; and the firmament shows His handiwork.

Day unto day uttereth speech, and night unto night shows knowledge.

There is no speech nor language, where their voice is not heard.

Their line is gone out through all the earth, and their words to the end of the world.

In them has He set a tabernacle for the sun,

Which is as a bridegroom coming out of his chamber, and rejoices as a strong man to run a race.

His going forth is from the end of the heaven,

and his circuit unto the ends of it:
and there is nothing hid from the heat thereof.

The law of the Lord is perfect,
converting the soul:
the testimony of the Lord is sure,
making wise the simple.

The statutes of the Lord are right,
rejoicing the heart:
the commandment of the Lord is pure,
enlightening the eyes.

The fear of the Lord is clean,
enduring for ever:
the judgments of the Lord are true
and righteous altogether.

More to be desired are they than gold,
yea, than much fine gold:
sweeter also than honey and the honeycomb.

Moreover by them is your servant
warned:
and in keeping of them there is great reward.

Who can understand his errors?
cleanse me from secret faults.

Keep back Your servant also from
presumptuous sins;
let them not have dominion over me:
then shall I be upright,
and I shall be innocent

from the great transgression.

Let the words of my mouth,
and the meditation of my heart,
be acceptable in Your sight,
O Lord, my strength, and my redeemer.

Chapter Three

EVALUATION . . . of the WORD

The second big word in Bible memorizing is *Evaluation.* Why should I memorize *Scripture?* There are other things one could memorize. It's all right for others to memorize Scripture, but I'm just too busy. That's the big question that must be answered as we evaluate all that is involved in the pursuit of memorizing the Word of God.

Some years ago, the executive officer of a denomination with headquarters in the Midwest region wrote me to ask concerning some details regarding Scripture memorization. He stated that many of their people were suggesting memorizing the Scriptures, and then, in what seemed like a distressing manner, he said that they had not even developed a *rationale* for Bible memorization. He proceeded to ask me if we had a *rationale* and would I mind telling him what it was, both from the *biblical* point of view, the *educational* point of view and the *psychological* point of view.

I studied the matter, and then to make sure that I was on the same wave length, I looked it up in the dictionary and found that "rationale" means, "the fundamental reasons for something." The letter was somewhat unusual, but basically it was *sad*. Here is a large group of people with a leading officer who does not seem to know the value and the basic reasons for memorizing Scripture.

After a week or two I answered briefly, as follows: "At the risk of being simplistic, I want to say that we do have a rationale for memorizing Scripture which was established by God Himself thousands of years ago. Here it is: (1) "Thy Word" — that's the biblical aspect of it. It is God's infallible, inerrant Word that we are dealing with. (2) "Have I hid in mine heart" —

that's the educational or disciplinary part of it. It takes real effort to store up the Word of God in the mind and heart. (3) *"That I might not sin against You* — that's the psychological or spiritual aspect of it.

Oh yes, I said some other things to him and tried to encourage him in the best way I knew how, to definitely challenge his people to memorize the Word of God and that nothing could be more profitable in their spiritual experience than assimilating individually the Word that comes from God. I think I concluded the letter by saying, *"'Your Word'* — that's the best possession; *'have I hid in my heart'* — that's the best place; *'that I might not sin against You'* — that's the best purpose."

We need to memorize Scripture because it is truly God's Word. We need only to recall what we learned in the previous chapter. This Word comes from God, and it is God's personal message to each one of us. As we meditate upon it, we learn what He wants us to know, what pleases Him and what His will is for each one of us every step of the way. Through the Word the unregenerate are "made wise unto salvation" (2 Tim. 3:15), and by it, the believers are disciplined and instructed (2 Tim. 3:16, 17). Indeed there are other writings which command our attention. The thought-provoking words of great men often commend themselves to us. The choice gems of literature which have lived for generations can be very satisfying to the soul. But all these are like the grass of the field which quickly withers and like the flower of the field which soon fades away.

Here is how Job evaluated God's Word: *"I have esteemed the words of his mouth more than my necessary food"* (23:12).

Most believers heartily agree with *Robert E. Lee's* succinct assessment of divine revelation when he said, "The Bible is a book in comparison with which all others in my eyes are of minor importance, and which in all my perplexities and distresses have never failed to give me light and strength."

Mrs. Ruth Taylor of Prairie Village, Kansas writes, "In my life, trouble comes from time to time, but always from my Father's hand to be beneficial to me. If I keep my mind centered on God—His Word and His promises—I have perfect peace. This is one great benefit from memorizing God's Word and I praise Him for the opportunity to memorize in your plan."

The value of receiving God's Word into our hearts is stressed strongly throughout the Book of Proverbs. We read: "My son, if you will receive my words, and hide my commandments with you; so that you incline your ear unto wisdom, and apply your heart to understanding; yea, if you cry after knowledge, and lift up your voice for understanding; if you seek her as silver, and search for her as for hid treasures; then shall you understand the fear of the Lord, and find the knowledge of God. For the Lord gives wisdom: out of His mouth comes knowledge and understanding" (Prov. 2:1-6). We are instructed to receive the Word of God and ponder it with diligence as the one who "sat at Jesus' feet, and heard His word" (Lu. 10:39). "The ear must be turned away from the sounds of earthly pleasures, the din of worldliness, the voice of human speculation, and must listen attentively to communications from the spiritual and eternal" (*D. Thomas*).

The child of God is instructed to seek the wisdom of God as silver, "not merely scrape the surface and get a few superficial scraps of knowledge" *Fausset* suggests, "but dig deep, and far, and wide. 'The treasures' are 'hidden' by God, not in order to keep them back from us, but to stimulate our faith and patient perseverance in seeking for them."

We Must Memorize the Scriptures

We must memorize the Scriptures *because God instructs us and commands us to do so*: "These words which I command you this day shall be in your heart" (Deut. 6:6). This was God's directive for the children of Israel. It is equally God's directive for all of His children today. The exhortation is developed further when God says, "Therefore shall you lay up these my words in your heart and in your soul" (Deut. 11:18). This means that we are to *store up* the eternal revelation of God methodically; *treasure up* the precious promises eagerly, and be able to use them effectively.

We memorize the Scriptures *because we need them so urgently* in every area of life and service. We are never sufficient of ourselves (2 Cor. 3:5). We need the Word of God in our hearts and on our lips to keep us from failure (Josh. 1:8). We need this Word to dwell richly in our hearts throughout the day and in the night seasons so that we might be protected from Satan's fiery darts and the adverse influences of the ungodly (Ps. 1:1, 2).

I recall a very personal experience when we visited my parents many years ago in Arborg, Manitoba, Canada. I noticed that my mother, who was bedfast with arthritis, kept the light on in her room all night long. I asked her why and her reply was that she was troubled by the darkness. I asked her how many verses of the Bible she knew from memory. My parents were saved late in life; my mother thought for a moment and then with sadness on her face, she said, "I do not believe I can recall any Bible verses." So I quoted to her Psalm 27:1, "The Lord is my light and my salvation; whom shall I fear? The Lord is the strength of my life; of whom shall I be afraid?" and then I said to her, "Mother, reciting that verse of Scripture in the darkest night will do much more for you than all the lights in the house." We slowly recited the verse together. Then we read and meditated on Psalm 23, and I suggested that she try to memorize that Psalm.

Don't you know, dear friends, that there are hundreds and thousands of people in our churches and in our land who are troubled by the darkness of the night just like my mother and they desperately need to have the Word of God tucked away in their hearts, which they can recall with great blessing and "light."

Reading the Word of God is good; studying it is better; but memorizing it is the best of all because this enables us to have it instantly accessible for every time of need. The person whose "delight is in the law of the Lord," "shall be like a tree planted by the rivers of water. . . and whatsoever he does shall prosper." Memorizing the Word enables a person not only to meditate on it day and night but gives him a continual hidden resource of strength.

When the Word is allowed to permeate our thinking and control our decisions it becomes profitable in every area of our spiritual progress. It helps to keep us from error (Matt. 22:29). It teaches, warns and keeps the child of God from backsliding (Ps. 19:11; 37:31). It causes him to enjoy progressive spiritual growth (1 Pet. 2:2); it strengthens his faith (Rom. 10:17), his prayer life (Jn. 15:7), his witness (1 Pet. 3:15) and his worship (Jn. 4:24).

Memorizing Scripture is something that Satan resists with all his might and it's a tremendous battlefield. I never consider lightly the objections or excuses that people make when approached with this subject.

Resistance and Problems

Take the *businessman* for instance who

considers the matter of memorizing Scripture
and wonders if he is actually just too busy to do
it. He is pressed with duties and his mind is
occupied with the many decisions that he has to
make from day to day. Yet, as he recognizes
that all of his time—day and night—belongs to
the Lord (Ps. 74:16), he proceeds to rearrange
his priorities, puts the claims of the Lord "first"
(Matt. 6:33); strangely enough, he finds the necessary time for memorizing the Word. Then he
discovers a new sense of the Lord's presence and
power which begin to control his life, and the
Lord's wisdom begins to show itself in the af-
fairs of his business.

The *high school girl* is really pushed with
her schoolwork, piano, home chores and other
activities, and she really wonders if she will
have the time to memorize God's Word in a systematic way like she had done for a good many
years before. Parents and pastor may encourage her, but she must decide this for herself.
She realizes that now she is going to be facing
opposition to the things of God from the secular world much more than when she was
younger; she realizes the need for that daily
spiritual discipline in the Word and a close relationship with the Lord. She knows the importance of meditating upon the Word of God

in her daily quiet time. So she prays after this manner and often with tears, "Lord, the schoolwork is hard and I have many things that crowd my daily schedule, but I do not want to neglect your Word. Please help me as I memorize it and meditate upon it. Help me so that it will not hinder my schoolwork and make me a true witness for yourself in my big mission field—the high school."

Yes, the Lord does enable and help because it is His will that each one of us think upon His Word regularly. The high school girl continues to memorize the Scriptures systematically all through those difficult years. She keeps up with all the other pursuits, she has a very real witness for the Lord with the students and faculty, she tries to put the things of God "first," and God "adds" the other things for her even as He promises. Her grades were surprising in that she was in the top fifteen percent of the school, and her vibrant personality and witness became noticeable so that she had a major part in the graduation exercises of the large city high school.

Now the story about *Sally Ellen Coleman*, Louisiana, who was promoted to glory on September 6, 1980,—*Mrs. Lois Coleman*, her mother, writes as follows: "I have completed the summer memory book, 'Praising the Lord.' It has been a blessing to my heart. It has met a real need.

"You see, the Lord called my just grown-up daughter home to Himself. And, although I know His ways are perfect, *there are times when praise comes hard.* This little book set it all in order and helped me to praise the Lord, not the circumstances, thru it all."

Sally Ellen Coleman was a radiant Christian — a lovely young lady. Her mother enrolled her in our Elementary Book 1 when she was only four years of age, and she never missed a year until she had to drop out in Collegiate Book 5 because of the brain tumor that took her earthly life. She completed the Elementary Series, the Intermediate Series, the High School Series and was on the 5th book of the Collegiate Series. This represented 17 Memory Books containing over 1700 choice Bible verses.

The Word of God prepares a person for life or for death. Sally wanted to live, but was not afraid of dying. She and her mother wept together as the "silent killer" advanced, but she could say, "It's O. K., Mom."

"She never complained"; her mother

said, "she never was afraid." Her earthly body died on Saturday, September 6, 1980, but she is indeed "more alive than ever!"

The *mother* with two or three small children is hard put to know what to do. She definitely wants the children to hide the word of God in their hearts while they are young, but she does not think that she will be able to help them and pursue the memorization herself on the adult level. But she was stung with conviction one day when the youngest child, *Laura Lee,* said to her, "Mother, why don't you and daddy memorize the Bible like we do?" That did it: she knew that the parents must set the right example for their children. "That did it," as *Jack Stem* can testify. Every parent soon learns that all the effort expended in training the child to memorize Scripture is the finest investment in the life of the child. The benefits are about as infinite as is the Word of God itself.

"Train up a child in the way he should go, and when he is old, he will not depart from it" (Prov. 22:6).

Dr. Arnold Burron, retired professor of education at the University of Northern Colorado writes, "This statement by Almighty God, the Author and Finisher of our faith, is an unbreakable promise, a written guarantee of success, a guarantee that cannot be rescinded. It is a promise that, if we attend to our one, major, most significant task as parents, *we cannot fail.* Regardless of what appears to be taking place throughout our child's life as he or she grows into adulthood, such as antisocial or even worse — illegal activities, immoral behavior, personal adjustment problems, or other spiritual adversities, we do not need to fear for our child's eternal salvation if we have obeyed God and followed His command. If we have 'trained our child in the way he should go,' God does not say:

'It is *likely* that when he is old he will not depart from it,' or 'it is *probable* that when he is old he will not depart from it,' or '*chances are,* there's a statistically significant tendency that. . .' or even that it is *desirable* to train a child, because it 'enhances the possibilities that he may someday reflect his early training,' or some other platitudinous empty conjecture.

"God says that if we train him up in the way he should go, when he is old HE WILL NOT DEPART FROM IT! Think of it! Guaranteed success!"

But we must not overlook the *pastor*! Having served as a pastor for a number of years myself, I am most sympathetic with the spiritual battles that the pastor is continually engaged in. Yet, we have to face realities. He is the one who urges the members of the congregation to read the Bible regularly and to follow some definite system of memorizing portions of it. Yet so often he himself is not doing it. Well, it's because he is so busy taking care of the flock which involves preparing many sermons and counseling with individuals day and night.

However, the conscientious pastor will soon confess that no matter how busy he may be with the work of the Lord, he must take time regularly to drink in the Word of God for himself. He will soon discover that reading and studying the Scriptures is certainly needful but the thing that will lend the greatest power to his ministry is the methodical memorization of the Word not just for the sake of the messages but feeding on it for his personal resource and profit. Indeed, his messages will acquire a keen edge and will be charged with such divine power that his own heart will be blessed and strengthened as he proclaims the Word to others.

I just received a letter from *Rev. Jerry Sheffield*, a pastor in Italy, Texas, who comfirms these thoughts; he said, "Since becoming acquainted with your systematic memorization of Scripture, it has become a way of life with us. It has been greatly used of the Lord in my own life as well as the lives of my wife and children. It is such a joy to see our children learn His word and hide it in their hearts. . . . As pastor, another great joy is seeing the people grow through the ministry of the Word. It truly is one of the most helpful and productive means for spiritual growth."

"To the Bible men will return," said *Matthew Arnold*, scholar and educator of the nineteenth century, "because they cannot do without it; because happiness is our being's end and aim, and happiness belongs to righteousness, and righteousness is revealed in the Bible. For this simple reason men will return to the Bible, just as a man who tried to give up food, thinking it was a vain thing and that he could do without it, would return to food."

Put it down, friend, put it down in letters bold and clear so you can always see it and be reminded that it is God's will for you to memorize Scripture. There must be not only a willingness to do it but a thoughtful, sincere determination to pursue it. You will be blessed and you will be an "example of the believers" (1 Tim. 4:12).

"The wise men are ashamed, they are dismayed and taken: lo, they have rejected the word of the Lord; and what wisdom is in them?" (Jer. 8:9).

Brethren, these are the conditions under which we live these days! The wise men of the world are confused and are "taken" by their own predictions and proclamations. We know for a fact that there is no wisdom apart from the Word of God. Some of the worldly-wise act as if we had never received a revelation and the needed wisdom from God Himself. Jeremiah points that out when he says, "Behold, they say unto me, Where is the word of the Lord?" and then, as if with a forceful wave of his arm and with raised voice, he says, "*Let it come now!*" (Jer. 17:15). Let the Word of God sweep across this land and throughout the world *now*. If ever it was needed in the hearts of young and older, it is *now*.

Chapter Four

ORGANIZATION . . .
for memorizing the WORD

The person who has definitely purposed to memorize Scripture immediately faces the question as to what portion of the Bible he is going to work on. Then comes the matter of schedule and the discipline required.

It is a universal fact that unless we have a workable plan including a specific schedule, we will not get very far with memorizing the Word irrespective of how highly we may value it or how urgently we may desire to do it. We seldom accomplish anything worthwhile in any field of endeavor without a definite plan. This is true in business. This is true in school and at home. It is certainly just as true in every area of our spiritual progress.

After careful thought and prayer, you have to decide what portion of the Bible you want to commit to memory and adopt a plan which works best for you.

Various Plans for Memorizing

There are several ways in which Bible memorizing may be followed:

(1) One plan that some people follow is that of memorizing certain verses in connection with the daily Bible reading and quiet time. The most significant verses are checked or underlined and an effort is made to memorize them. This seems to work for some people very nicely. However, for the most part, although it seems good in theory, it fails in actual practice. I recall a statement from a friend in Kansas a few years ago, "I tried to memorize verses as a part of my devotions each day, but I felt lost in the project. I realized that I needed some specific guidelines" (*Kathleen Regehr*).

(2) Memorizing a certain chapter or an entire Book in the Bible is often undertaken. I

tried it a number of times but seldom got very far with it. This has some real advantages. There is generally a sequence of thought, and there is no question but that following such a plan, you will understand the verses in that chapter or book better as you memorize all the verses in their context. This significant factor must not be overlooked. A few people succeed in memorizing all the Psalms, some absorb other long books or even the entire New Testament, and they do so with great profit.

Thomas Cranmer, the first Protestant Archbishop of Canterbury, memorized the whole of the New Testament on his journey to Rome. *Frances Ridley Havergal*, one of the outstanding hymn writers of England who lived only 42 years (1836-1879), committed to memory all of the New Testament, the entire book of Psalms, and the book of Isaiah while she was still a teenager. Later she added all the Minor Prophets. She had in memory a total of 12,935 Bible verses.

Although this plan has some distinct advantages, it has to be organized and implemented with systematic effort. *John Ruskin* tells about the outstanding chapters of the Bible which his mother selected for him to memorize. Among them was Psalm 119, which is the longest chapter in the Bible. Not only did she insist upon daily pursuit of it, but it had to be done word-perfect and recited with expression so as to indicate that he really understood what he had memorized. He said that as a boy he just knew that he would always dislike the Bible and that the one chapter that he would most assuredly detest would be Psalm 119. On the contrary, he attributed his greatest achievements in life to the reverence of the Scriptures that his mother had instilled in him as a boy.

"All that I have taught of art," he said, "everything that I have written, every greatness that has been in any thought of mine, whatever I have done in my life, has simply been due to the fact that when I was a child, my mother daily read with me a part of the Bible, and daily made me learn a part of it by heart." Elsewhere he stated that although he loved the entire Bible, yet the one Scripture which was like a river of delight to him was Psalm 119. To quote him exactly—"It is strange that of all the pieces of the Bible which my mother taught me, that which cost me the most to learn, and which was to my child's mind most repulsive—the 119th Psalm—has now become of all the most precious to me in its overflowing and glorious passion of love for the law of God."

(3) Typing or printing the desired Bible verses on small cards has been used by many quite successfully in memorizing the Word. The Scripture text generally printed on one side and the reference on the other. Many individuals have developed such for themselves, but it has been best perfected and used by the *Navigators* and by the *Young Life Campaign*, who have arranged the verses under topical headings and assembled them in packets for handy use. This plan has certain merits and many, particularly adults, have been blessed in following such a system.

(4) Another plan is that of memorizing key verses in the books of the Bible and in many of the outstanding chapters. This also facilitates learning the contents of the Bible inasmuch as the key verses often shed light on the entire chapter or book.

Whatever the plan one undertakes to follow, there must be a set schedule and that personal discipline of doing it methodically and regularly until it becomes a part of one's life, just like certain habits and routines in other areas of life.

(5) The most effective Bible memorizing plan, I believe, is that where the desired Scriptures are organized under practical and instructive topical headings, so that we may re-

call Bible truths most promptly in the varied situations that come up in life. Scripture organized by assignment headings enable a person to associate them with the particular topic and be able to recall them more readily. A pharmacist's assistant will learn the names of medicines in the shop much sooner when they are properly labelled and arranged on the shelves in an orderly manner. So, the topical headings make for a connection of the verses; they enable a person to memorize them more readily and remember them longer.

Now, what plan to follow and how to proceed is really the big concern that every parent, every pastor, school principal and Christian leader who feels responsible for others has to face and has to come up with a real conclusion, not only for his own sake but for the sake of the people whom he is leading.

This is not a simple decision because there is such a variety of people under his administration, including degrees of progress spiritually, as well as age levels, etc.

Practical Use of Scripture Illustrated

Although there are advantages to learning the Scriptures by chapters or by books as stated previously, the fact is that in our everyday life we seldom use them that way. We do not normally recall or meditate upon large portions of the Bible in the practical situations that arise. This is true in the experience of children as well as adults. We generally lay hold of a verse or two in that moment of need or that unexpected opportunity for witness.

The main purpose for memorizing the Word of God is certainly not just for the sake of learning and knowledge, but in order that we might be better equipped and strengthened in our Christian walk and service. Having the quickening Word instantly accessible is of inestimable value. It is so wonderful and so spirit-energizing to be able to recall it and use it in answer to specific questions that arise and to meet the particular needs that come up in our lives throughout the day and in the night seasons.

A good example of this idea is the way our Lord Himself used the Scriptures. When He had been without food for forty days, He was tempted by Satan to change the stones into bread and satisfy His hunger. Christ did not recite to him the book of Deuteronomy nor did He even cover a chapter. He simply took part of Deuteronomy 8:3 and said, "It is written, man

shall not live by bread alone, but by every word
that proceeds out of the mouth of God" (Matt.
4:4). When Satan, who apparently knows Scripture and know its power perhaps better than we
do (Lu. 8:12), resorted to using it, our Lord simply recalled another Scripture and said, "It is
written again" (Matt. 4:7). Reading the book of
Acts, it is amazing to see how much of God's
Word the apostles had stored up in their memories and how effectually they drew upon different portions of it in their witness and in their
messages.

Underlying Philosophy

This is the underlying philosophy in the
organization and development of the fifty-three
memory books which the Lord enabled me to
develop for all ages. This concept guided the
careful preparation of the assignment headings
and the selection of the most appropriate Scriptures for each particular heading in the different Memory Books. The vital principle always
kept in mind was how best to help the child, the
young person or the adult in the use of the Word
of God in his daily Christian life.

Eleven Series of Memory Work for all Ages

There are eleven memory plans for the
different age levels. I would like to introduce two

of the Memory Books at this point. One is the Elementary Memory Book 5, which is designed for children ages 9 through 11. The Scriptures deal with the different aspects of the child's Christian walk and witness; the title of the book is *"Pleasing God."* There are twelve assignments in the book with headings as follows:

1) Pleasing God in My Thought
2) Pleasing God in My Walk
3) Pleasing God in My Talk
4) Pleasing God in My Trials
5) Pleasing God in My Training
6) Pleasing God in My Trusting
7) Pleasing God as I Play
8) Pleasing God as I Pray
9) Pleasing God as I Obey
10) Pleasing God as I Work
11) Pleasing God as I Witness
12) Pleasing God as I Worship

In this book there are six carefully selected verses for each assignment, which the child memorizes in one week's time.

From the Basic Adult Series, I am presenting here Book 2, titled *"Walk in the Light"* which has fifteen assignments. Seven appropriate verses are included under each assignment heading:

1) Uninterrupted Communion
2) Unsuppressed Confession
3) Unreserved Surrender
4) Unwavering Devotion
5) Unceasing Prayer
6) Delighting in His Word
7) Responding to His Will
8) Rejoicing in His Praise
9) Abounding in His Strength
10) Living in the Spirit
11) The Function of Faith
12) The Glory of Tribulation
13) The Light of Discernment
14) The Fellowship of Love
15) The Continual Allowance

Well over a million children, young people and adults have memorized the Scriptures in this systematic way by the use of these Memory Books. God's Word does not return to Him void, and the spiritual blessings received have been most far-reaching and can never be fully described this side of heaven. Thousands of testimonies and expressions of appreciation have been received. Here are one or two with just the right word for our thoughts under organization of a memory plan: "The verses from Basic Adult Book 1 and 2 have helped me so much, both in my personal life and in dealing with others. Though these same verses have always been available to me in the Bible, I would never have memorized them without a course such as you are presenting" (*Mrs. W. J. Ebert, Richmond, VA*).

"I have greatly appreciated learning verses in the systematic manner because of the way the verses are organized by topics; this arrangement not only makes memorizing easier for me but helps explain the significance of the verses" (*Dr. Justin Long, Lanham, MD*).

The Use of Incentives

The use of incentives for memorizing Scripture generally proves very helpful, particularly with children, who usually do not recognize the value of Scriptures themselves. Some small incentives can be used during the learning process. These may include the parental word of approval, the special dessert, the trip to the zoo, etc. One cannot help but wonder what incentives *Mr. and Mrs. Jesse* used when they encouraged David to memorize Scripture! Perhaps they offered him a special trip to Elim (Ex. 15:27), or promised him a brand new harp when he completed the "Moses Series" of the Bible memorization! As we read Psalm 19, Psalm 119 and others we know that as an adult he recognized the fact that the wonderful Word of God itself was his greatest reward.

C. H. *Spurgeon*, of London and world fame, tells of how his grandmother encouraged him to memorize the Scriptures and hymns by giving him certain amounts of money. His grandfather, he said, paid him a shilling for killing rats in his business warehouse. Spurgeon recalled that he enjoyed killing rats much more than he did the memorization of the Scripture and made more money at it, but it was the storing up of God's Word and the good old hymns which proved most helpful in his lifelong ministry. Spurgeon's sermons continue to be reprinted and one has only to read them to find out that the reason why their richness endures lies in the fact that they are so thoroughly "Bibline."

Recognition of good Bible memory work may include recitation of the Scriptures in services, attractive achievement cards, diplomas, personalized plaques and trophies. A well-planned system of rewards which are faithfully given out at certain intervals, as promised, serves as a great inducement to continue with the work not only on the part of children but young people and adults as well. The rewards should be selected with great care, and whether they are books, plaques, recordings, games, novelties or other items, they should be attractive, appropriate for the particular age level and, above all else, they should bear a clear spiritual message and witness.

Academic credits in school can prove to be a significant reward. Thus the rewards serve a double purpose. They provide incentives for memorizing the Word and they render a spiritual ministry in themselves. The offer of a few days or a week at a Bible camp as reward for completion of prescribed Bible memory work does wonders with some people, both young and older. A church or school that desires to excel in Bible memorizing will do well to give adequate consideration and expense to the incentives system.

We have read hundreds of testimonies from people of all ages and from all parts of the world which tell of the tremendous significance and blessing of the rewards received as a result of memorizing the Scriptures.

I came across this one from Montgomery, Alabama: "I am in the midst of reading one of my rewards, 'The Teacher's Manual — Basis for the Christian Life.' I am an avid reader and have read many heart-warming, thought-provoking study books, but Sir, I have never run across a manual like this which contains so much meat; I find myself literally devouring its contents due in large measure, I think, to its simple, concise explanation of the Gospel of John" (*Miss Peggy Smith*).

Schedule and Requirements

When shall a person memorize God's Word? This is a question that comes up at once and in the case of churches and schools this requires a great deal of consideration. A thorough organization of a Scripture memorizing plan will not overlook the establishment of a set schedule for the learning and reciting of the prescribed number of selected verses. These *requirements* of learning and reciting must be diligently maintained or else the entire system falls apart.

A good plan of committing the eternal Word to memory is like a school. It is taken seriously. The learning goes on day after day and the students submit to the required tests at the stated times. This makes for a disciplinary type of learning and brings about wonderful results. Participants in the system which uses our Memory Books are to spend most of the week in learning the given number of verses in each assignment and they are required to recite the assignment at a stated time during the weekend.

Deciding on the best segment of weeks for the memorization course and the arranging of a definite recitation schedule must be developed with studied attention to all that is involved. The importance of adhering to the recitation schedule cannot be over-estimated. Such requirements in a Scripture memory program are just as essential as are the various requirements prescibed and followed in any well-ordered school. The details on recitations, including the amount of time spent in preparation, the standard of perfection in the reciting and the careful attention to the scheduled time for each recitation should be clearly spelled out in a written manual for those who supervise the work and those who hear the recitations in any school, church or other groups.

I can say without any fear of contradiction that having a well-organized Scripture memory plan, employing thoroughly the idea of recognition and helpful rewards and requiring the recitiation of the assignments at stated times, helps most folks to do very gratifying work in storing in their memory the Word of God. Over 75% of the participants usually finish

62

the year's work.

Let me introduce you to a couple of individuals who have been exceedingly pleased with this Bible memorizing system. One is *Mrs. Frank Toman*, New Dundee, Ontario, who wrote, "Personally, I find your way of memorizing just what I need for both Bible knowledge and meditation and instruction. As a family we have been memorizing for twelve years. It sure helps when Mom and Dad (or both) are in it, too. The children realize it is important because the parents consider it to be of great value. This gives us as parents an informal opportunity to discuss spiritual truths with the children personally. (They are past the age when you read to them at night!)."

The other is *Mr. Harold R. Stephens*, a business man in Memphis, whose comprehensive statement should prove quite challenging, particularly to businessmen who are so often pressed with many cares,

"I never cease to marvel at the tremendous way that God is using this systematic method of Scripture memorization to enlighten darkened minds to their need of the Savior, and to afford the believer a better understanding of all the unlimited resources with which he is provided, as a member of the body of Christ.

"I can truthfully say, that as a result of my participation in this wonderful program of hiding God's Word away in my heart, I have a better understanding, and a greater love and respect for the inspired Word of God, than could have been derived from any other method I might have followed.

"I will forever be grateful to God for having provided such an effective program and the human instruments for the initiation of this wonderful program, and for its perpetuation for these many years.

"My prayer is that God will continue to use Dr. Woychuk and all his helpers greatly in their efforts to strengthen the body of Christ, and that all those who participate in memorizing according to this plan may be greatly blessed of the Lord, and made to continually grow in the grace and the knowledge of our Lord and Savior Jesus Christ."

Practical Suggestions for Learning and Remembering

As you work at it, your own ideas will probably serve you the best. I am listing a few suggestions which have proved themselves with many people.

1) Read carefully the entire assignment of verses you have purposed to memorize that week, and ask God to help you as you undertake to commit His Word to memory. Like the Psalmist, pray "Open my eyes, that I may

behold wondrous things out of Your law" (Ps. 119:18). God will certainly help you because this is precisely what He wants you to do.

2) First *study* the Scriptures so that you may understand their meaning. If you are working on selected verses arranged under topics, look them up in your Bible and read the whole passage from which the verses are taken. It is difficult to memorize something which you do not understand.

3) Do not neglect to learn the references. It not only helps you to locate it in the Bible, but it will serve to help you recall it in many ways — while driving, just before going to sleep, etc.

4) Try to make the verses you are memorizing form a definite connection with the main thought of the chapter *or* the topical heading.

5) Writing the verses out thoughtfully; writing them out one time is generally considered as good for remembering as reading them over four or five times.

6) It will prove helpful to read the verses out loud and doing so with real expression.

7) Recording the verses on cassettes proves helpful in many ways — while driving, just before going to sleep, etc.

8) "Whole learning" is considered

about twenty percent more efficient than "part learning." Go through the entire passage or assignment, or at least through an entire verse. After the framework of the Scripture has emerged, the rest of the words will begin to fit in more meaningfully and more easily. You'll tend to be remembering thoughts while concentrating on the exact words.

9) Better work is usually done in short periods of time, with breaks for casual reflection on the verses in order to help fix the material in your mind. The break will enable you to resume the concentration with fresh vigor.

10) The secret of really enjoying the verses is to "over-learn" them in the first place. When you think you already know it, just put a little extra time on it. Fasten it thus more permanently in your "recall cassette" and in the sub-conscious.

11) The grand secret of remembering is reviewing the verses with a purpose.

Some of these suggestions and others are developed more fully in the succeeding chapters.

Helping Children

In teaching the verses to children, parents,

teachers and Christian workers utilize various ideas which seem to work best for them. Preschool children particularly require adult help. Some suggestions that have come to our attention are included here:

1) Read the verses aloud, and do so with expression and enthusiasm. Explain the meaning of the verses in simple terms. Go over the verses with the child while eating, before bed, while working, while walking together and while riding in the car (Deut. 6:7). Most parents memorize the verses along with the child.

2) Do not insist that the child repeat the verse or verses each time.

3) *Mrs. Claire Lynn* and other mothers have told me how they have put the verses to simple tunes which they sing with the child over and over again. Be sure that the exact words of Scripture are used. In this way the child learns faster and remembers longer. We now have tapes and CDs featuring melodies on the verses in the Bible Forget-Me-Nots, ABC and I Am and the "Prayer" memory book in the Premier Adult series.

4) Read the child's verses to him each morning while he is eating breadkfast. Read them again at family devotions in the morning or in the evening.

5) Discuss the meaning of the verses in the home circle. This will help the child to relate the verses to his activities and needs. He will be very pleased when he begins to contribute something from his own store of verses.

6) Acting out verses which lend themselves for such a purpose aids the learning process. For example in Psalm 1, you can "walk," "stand" and "sit."

7) Filling in the missing words can be a *delightful way* of learning for children.

8) Turning off the TV, the radio, the internet and scheduling a set time for learning Bible verses will prove helpful. Occasionally it may be that neighborhood friends will either "want to" go home or "want to" learn the verses also.

9) Communicate your approval of the child's work. Words of praise are always a strong motivating force.

10) When an older child lacks the initiative to learn his verses himself, you will want to work with him and encourage him. Suggest that he read the verses out loud to you a time or two. He may be suprised that by then he can recite them.

11) Always strive to make each Scripture

reveal something about the Lord Jesus Christ and the child's relation to Him. Many children are saved even as they memorize the Word in their early years. Then there is the life-long process of growing for them and for us. "As new-born babes, desire the sincere milk of the word, that you may grow thereby" (1 Pet. 2:2).

12) "It is good to think of memorization of Scripture as an investment in the life of a young child. The benefits are as infinite as the Word of God itself" (*Martha Evans*, Arlington, VA).

Chapter Five

ASSIMILATION . . . of the Word

In the previous chapters we have been introduced to a particular system of Bible memorizing. The inspired Word of the living God is now before us arranged and printed attractively in memory book portions easy to take. What shall we do with it? We may choose to admire it and just let it alone. We may express sincere appreciation for the way it seems to bless other lives. But this will be of no profit to us unless we heed the command of God as given through the prophet Isaiah, "Eat ye that which is good and let your soul delight itself in fatness" (55:2).

Literally, it means eat that which is supremely good and let your soul have a spiritual banquet.

This is an imperative command to assimilate, to take in the Word of God; "to comsume and incorporate into the mind." Just as eating food results in the desired good effect upon the body, so the mental-spiritual ingestion of the Scripture provides the needed spiritual nourishment for the inner man of the Christian.

How can a person actually "eat" the Word of God?

The prophet Jeremiah spoke about assimilation of the Word of God when he said exultingly, "Your words were found and I did eat them; and Your word was unto me the joy and rejoicing of mine heart; for I am called by Your name, O Lord God of hosts" (15:16). The books of Moses apparently had been buried for some time in the ruins of the temple until the reign of King Josiah, when the temple was repaired and restored. There, in the rubbish the workers found the law of Moses.

The king "read" in their ears all the words of the book of the covenant which was found in the house of the Lord. And then the record continues, "the king stood by a pillar, and made a covenant before the Lord. . . . And all the people stood to the covenant" (2 Kings 23:2, 3). Jeremiah may have very well been among those people who dedicated their lives to the Lord along with Josiah, following the reading of God's Word. Jeremiah was thrilled with the Word of God and didn't just admire it or nibble on it; he ate big mouthfuls of it. The word caused much rejoicing in the Lord on the part of the earnest prophet.

How May We Eat the Word

But how then can we truly "eat" the Word of God? It certainly does not mean eating the pages of the Bible, although a newspaper article sometime ago carried the story about the Australian nurse who had developed a craving for paper, tissues, newpaper sheets, blotting paper, pages from exercise books, etc. No, we are not instructed to eat the pages of the book, but as *C. H. Spurgeon* admonished, "It is blessed to eat into the very soul of the Bible until, at last, you come to talk in Scriptural language, and your spirit is flavored with the words of the Lord, so that your blood is *Bibline* and the very essence of the Bible flows from you."

How may we eat the Word of God, you ask?

It is certainly possible to assimilate some of the Word of God by hearing it read or proclaimed by others.

Much more spiritual nourishment will be gained by reading the Scriptures for yourself, not simply rushing through a chapter of words, but reading it leisurely and with a purpose. "Do not gallop through the Scriptures," *Joseph Parker* used to admonish young preachers, "Go slowly and look around." What does the rapid traveler see of the wayside flowers, or hear of the song of the birds?

The Word yields its precious secrets to the soul that moves with reverent and unhasty steps. In reading well, a person is comprehending, questioning, interpreting and comparing what he reads; it is a thought process which involves reasoning and remembering.

What we read is of inestimable importance because, consciously or unconsciously, it tends to shape our whole outlook on life. The German youth found the words of *Mein Kampf* and began eating them. In the course of a few years, *Hitler's* false philosophies incited their minds with unprecedented fanaticism — which brought destruction and death to millions and plunged their fatherland into ruin.

The people of Russia found the precepts of *Karl Marx* and ate them, and the godless plague of communism hung over half of the earth's population. For decades the teeming masses of China devoured the words of former chairman *Mao*, whose atheistic principles slaughtered missionaries and virtually blacked out completely the message of hope for the people of that land and the neighboring countries which they had conquered.

Oh, that we may have a hunger for the blessed Word of God and constantly be *renewed* in our minds so that we won't let the world's philosophies squeeze us into their mold.

"This is the real danger of the day," wrote *Mr. Fred Schuppe*, Arlington, VA, some years ago, "of being shaped or conformed to the world by all of the forces and pressures at work, such as the radio, TV, current magazines, newspapers, what the stream of society thinks, and the like. Practically everything we see, hear and read is contrary to the philosophy and thinking of the Word of God. The foregoing is negative. The positive is to be *transformed* by the renewing of our minds. I need to have my mind renewed, restored, constantly brought back to solid spiritual moorings by the Word of God and the Spirit of God. What does He say? What is His will? What are His purposes for me? God forbid that my thinking, my philosophy of life, my purpose for living should be molded by Wall Street, by Hollywood or by Paris stylists."

And the life where the Word of God is given preeminence is a life where the Word of God brings light and love and hope to an individual and to an entire country.

Read God's Word and your spirit will be introduced to the heart of God; memorize God's Word and His Spirit will begin to control your life and provide the right words to fit your needs as they arise from day to day. If a person actually develops a taste for the Word of God and submits to it, there will be a special intimacy between that person and the Father—between that person and the Son—and it would seem that in a very special way God the Father and God the Son will move into that life and take control of it (Jn. 14:23).

Still much more profit is gained from searching and studying the Scriptures in some methodical way. Sometimes, the message of God is hidden in a parable and we are to find it "in folds and garments of deftest imagery." Sometimes the light of the Word is concealed in words which the Lord spoke to another, and we are to listen with a kind of eager eavesdropping, to see if there is anything intended for our needy hearts. In studying the Word, we seek for truth not eloquence, we search after profit not subtle arguments, and best of all we yearn to find the Person of Christ on the sacred pages.

But the most effectual way of "eating" the Word of God, I think, is by memorizing it, so that it is not a transient thing like a caller who stays for an hour or so and continues on his journey; nay, this Word of Christ is made to remain in us, to settle down in us, to make its home in the inner soul and live in the deepest recesses of our being.

The Bible doesn't appeal to people who have gone without its essential nourishment for a long time. They have no appetite for it just like starving people show little enthusiasm for food because they have had nothing in their stomachs for such a long time.

Some years ago, I was impressed by the way a boy, about five years of age, was putting away the food in a restaurant in Blytheville Arkansas. He didn't really know how to use the knife and fork very well, but he obviously had a good appetite and wasted no time in eating all that was placed before him. I could not help but wish that all of us had such an appetite for the Word of God! We

76

would more eagerly heed the voice of God,—
"eat the good," —relish its sweetness (Ps. 19:10),
devour it with an aroused appetite and let it
"dwell" richly in our hearts. Let it become like
some royal presence, moving with authority and
grace, enriching everything it touches and transforming into spiritual gold all our thoughts, our
affections, our purposes and our actions.

Two Men Who Ate the Book

Two men in Scripture were actually
commanded to eat the pages which carried the
Word of God. They are Ezekiel (3:1-14) and
John (Rev. 10:1-11).

Ezekiel says, "Moreover he said unto me,
Son of man, eat that thou findest; eat this roll,
and go speak unto the house of Israel. So I
opened my mouth, and he caused me to eat that
roll" (Ezek. 3:1-2). He is not merely to take it
into his mouth, but he is to fill his belly there-
with; he is to take it into his innermost being,
and change it, as it were, into energy and blood.
The roll of God's Word to Israel was in the mouth
of Ezekiel "as honey for sweetness" (Ezek. 3:3),
but it carried him on a mission to which he "went
in bitterness, in the heat of my spirit" (Ezek. 3:14).

The power of God's Word in us is to
send us on errands and duties which are full

of hardships, trials and many a bitterness. Eating the Word is indeed pleasant to the taste, but it costs pain as the faithful believer or prophet goes out into an unsanctified world with the message of God in his heart.

John says, "I took the little book out of the angel's hand, and ate it up; and it was as honey: and as soon as I had eaten it, my belly was bitter. And he said unto me, Thou must prophesy again before many peoples" (Rev. 10:10, 11). Those precious title-deeds of the blessed inheritance were "sweet as honey" to John's mouth and they thrilled him with gladness, but when he had eaten it his "belly was bitter" because he had to prophesy concerning the scenes of blood and wrath to the dwellers upon earth. Such is the lot of those who eat the Word and hold faithfully to the holy document — many conflicts! much contradiction of sinners! laborious toils and unsuspecting dangers!

Though the eating of the roll and the book are symbolic the meaning of it is very real and true to the life in the experience of every believer. Jeremiah *ate* the words and found himself "in the stocks," and the "word of the Lord was made a reproach. . . . and a derision, daily." Jeremiah said, "I will not make mention of Him, nor speak any more in His name" (Jer. 20:1-9), I'll just keep quiet and mind my own business, he thought, but that's not the way it works. God's Word, when assimilated, becomes a mighty power within, and Jeremiah had eaten too much of the precious stuff, and soon realized that he could not keep it bottled up! "But His word was in mine heart as a burning fire shut up in my bones, and I was weary with forebearing, and I could not stay" (Jer. 20:9).

Reading and studying God's Word gets the person into the Word, but memorizing it gets the Word into the person, and there it becomes a major directive force in the spiritual unfolding and development of God's new creation.

"Eat the Good!"

The Bible is truly a wonderful Book. But as *General Gordon* used to say, "After all, the chief proof that the Bible is good food is the eating of it." Chemical investigation into the ingredients of a loaf of bread has its needful place, no doubt, but the analyst's household may starve, if they hesitate to feed upon it until the analysis has been completed to his entire satisfaction.

"Eat ye that which is good, and let your soul delight itself in fatness" (Isa. 55:2).

The big job is not only that of doing it ourselves, but how to get people in our churches, in our classes, in our Christian schools to assimilate the life-giving and life-nourishing Word! We are all keenly aware of the fact that we are living in an age when lawlessness abounds on every hand and it generally increases in proportion to the lack of reverence for the Word of God. The respect for the authority of the parents usually goes hand in hand with the respect that is shown for God and for His Word.

In Proverbs 6, we read about the seven things which the Lord hates:

"A proud look,

a lying tongue,

hands that shed innocent blood,

a heart that devises wicked imaginations,

feet that be swift in running to mischief,

a false witness that speaks lies,

he that sows discord among brethren" (16-19).

Then we note in the next verse (20), God's specific words of instruction: "My son, keep your father's commandment, and forsake not the law of your mother." This is certainly an explicit admonition for children to respect the instructions they receive from their parents, but it is interesting to note in verse 23 of that chapter that the father's "commandment" and the mother's "law" are the "lamp" and the "light" from the Lord Himself, and that their discipline and their teachings are "the way of life" which they have themselves obviously received from the Lord.

This instruction, though mediated through man, is of divine origin and enlightens the person who receives it. When the Apostle said, "Children obey your parents in the Lord for this is right" (Eph. 6:1), he was not promoting an arbitrary dominance of the parents, but he was specifically communicating the will of God.

Continually Nourished in the Word

Now, the question is, how can a person acquire the spiritual education in real life? I believe we find the answer in verse 21: "*Bind them continually upon your heart, and tie them about your neck.*" *Delitzch* suggests that these words, "bind them continually," are equivalent to the Latin "circumplicare," which means to wind round and round about an object. Just as the little "bouncer" in a golf ball is made more substantial and resilient with the winding of the many, many rounds of rubberized cord, so the Word of God increases the strength and agility of the person who assimilates the Scriptures *continually*.

This reminds us of the Word in Deuteronomy 6:6, 7: "And these words, which I command you this day, shall be in your heart. And you shall teach them diligently unto your children, and shall talk of them when you sit in your house, and when you walk by the way, and when you lie down, and when you rise up." The Word of God is to permeate and illuminate the person not just once in a while but throughout the whole day—"continually."

The Word of the living God is to be always present and affecting the whole of a person's life. The "heart" suggests that the Scriptures shall be vitally controlling our affections and decisions, and the "neck" suggests that the Scriptures will be an ornament adorning the moral character. The results are most gratifying. Here is what happens in the life of the person who is *continually* nourished with the Word (Prov. 6:21).

(1) *"When you go, it shall lead you"* — the Word treasured up in the heart shall be a sure guide. "And your ears shall hear a word

behind you, saying, This is the way, walk in it ..." (Isa. 30:21).

(2) *"When you sleep, it shall keep you"* — The Word stored up in the mind and heart will be your ever-present keeper throughout the night seasons, when His "speech shall distill as the dew" (Deut. 32:2) and afford you that perfect peace and security — "I will both lay me down in peace, and sleep: for you Lord, only make me dwell in safety" (Ps. 4:8).

(3) *"When you awake, it shall talk with you"* — when you arise in the morning, this Word ever present, will converse and commune with you. It will immediately make you aware of the Lord's nearness and companionship as you "stretch forth" your hands unto Him and say, "Cause me to hear your lovingkindness in the morning, For in you do I trust: cause me to know the way wherein I should walk, For I lift up my soul to you" (Ps. 143:6, 8).

Chapter Six

CONCENTRATION ... on the WORD

How then can we actually assimilate the Word of God?

As we have already observed, the best way to take in the Word of God is through the process of memorization. This calls for *concentration*. It means engaging your mental faculties on a particular subject. Memorizing has no real short cuts. It's just plain work. It calls for real diligence and is focused upon that which you desire to remember. Sloth, indolence and neglect will no more bless the mind with spiritual and intellectual riches than it will fill the hand with gain, the field with corn or the purse with treasure.

In the formation of man, God gave him a master control organ called the brain. This three and a half pounds of pinkish gray material embraces the marvelous mental capacities which at once distinguish man superlatively from all other forms of life.

Scientists tell us that the brain is composed of about 100 billion nerve cells called *neurons*, which are the functional units of the brain, and about ten times that many *glia* cells, which are largely "filler." All these cells are connected to each other by filaments and form the nerve network. These nerve cells receive and interpret the myriad bits of impulses pouring into the brain from the *sense* organs. The brain evaluates this information at memory's behest, determines the most suitable reactions and transmits messages out to the various parts of the body for action.

How exceedingly vital it is to have the memories adequately stocked with God's Word so that the sensory signals can be quickly interpreted and the actions determined in accordance with God's wisdom. The believer whose mind is saturated with the Word can respond quickly, with conviction, — "Thus saith the Lord," — and proceed unhesitatingly in doing the will of God.

The brain never sleeps; it remains continuously active and performs a bewildering variety of subtle functions. It regulates man's heart; it controls his body temperature; it switches his emotions on and off; it keeps him in touch with the world around him.

When we recognize the function of the brain, we really appreciate what the prophet meant when he said, "You will keep him in perfect peace whose mind is stayed on You, because he trusts in You" (Isa. 26:3). The human brain is the most fabulous "machine" in existence and compared with it the most advanced computer is only like a high-speed idiot. Man has split the atom, achieved unbelievable skills and leaped from his own terrestrial home to the moon, but he has yet to solve the mysteries of the brain as to its functions of thought, memory and self-consciousness.

Concentration is the backbone, the sustaining factor in memorization. You can be reading the Scriptures and trying to study them, while your mind quickly goes back to yesterday's problems or it jumps ahead to tomorrow's schedule, but when you *memorize* you have to exclude everything else and give it undivided attention. *Mrs. E. Hosback* has found to be true what most of us have experienced again and again. "Often," she said, "I find myself allowing cares and perplexities to fill my mind, but when I am learning these verses, such things are crowded out."

To some extent at least, we are all called upon to do some concentrating all along the way. We may classify the memorizing that is being done into three categories:

1) There is the *short-term memory*, lasting only a few seconds; every moment of our life, hundreds of impulses and impressions, stimulated by the senses, flow into the human brain, and are for the most part promptly forgotten. They did not seem to be of any material significance and failed to arouse any interest. *Everybody* does some memorizing on this level.

2) The second category is the *medium-term memory*, which lasts from a few minutes to a few hours or possibly extending into a day or two. This level of concentration enables a person to locate a certain house or remember a telephone number just long enough to dial it. This is probably the mediocre extent of concentration that is

utilized in "cramming" for an examination. Most people engage in this type of memorization also.

   3) The highest level of concentration is the *long-term memory*, where certain impressions and information entering the brain register strongly because of the *importance* and *usefulness* that is attached to them, or, as is so often true in the case of children, the *vividness* with which the information is presented. In this area of concentration, the person reacts with real enthusiasm and says to himself, consciously or unconsciously, I certainly want to remember this. He ponders on it intentionally. He takes time for that particular information to register permanently.

What is Concentration

   Concentration is our God-given power to be able to learn and retain what has been learned so that it can be recalled in the days and months to come. Of what value are all the intellectual and spiritual improvements if no effort is made to retain them and they are lost as soon as they are obtained? It is the blessed product of memory that enriches the mind and spirit by preserving what our disciplined labor has achieved. Without purposeful use of the memory, the soul of man is but a poor, destitute, naked being, with a meaningless blank spread over it, except for the fleeting ideas of the present moment. Such a life is but a wide-spread desert. Indeed, it is a fact that people who do not have the Word of God imprinted on their minds and hearts are living largely in a state of desolation, and the future spreads out before them like a barren wilderness.

Most Christians recognize not only the value of memorizing God's Word but they also see how essential it is in every area of the believer's life and service. They will readily admit this, but probably the main reason why they do not pursue it is because it involves *work*— determination, discipline, concentration. James speaks about the "double minded" man (1:8), which implies that he is distracted and divided in his thoughts, but "God has not given us the spirit of fear; but of power, and of love, and of a sound mind," (2 Tim. 1:7), yea a *mind of discipline*, as another version puts it.

We are all naturally a bit lazy and prone to idleness, or we will expose ourselves rather aimlessly to the entertainment, the lecturing or preaching by others. We simply resist the process of mental exercise that is necessary for memorizing. In this connection many people have rather eagerly grasped after artifical memory aids, which on the surface sound very promising.

Mnemonic Experiments

In the last half century there has been a rash of *mnemonics* which is a dignified term for memory improvement methodology. Around 1960, *Mr. O. W. Hayes* declared on the dust jacket of his book, *Your Memory*, "In just seven days you, too, can be a memory wizard." About the same time, *Mr. Harry Lorayne* advertised his *Instant Memory Course* on an LP recording. Then there were the visual aids for the memory instruction put out by Vicore, Inc., whose services were used for a short time by schools and government agencies. It was soon abandoned and its president, *Mrs. Elsie Carlson*, said that their system was "as good as any there is, but," she continued, "it took more time for students to learn the system than it was worth."

Probably the most ambitious undertaking in the realm of mental wizardry was that of *Dr. Bruno Furst*. It appeared on big-time TV shows and was written up in popular magazines. The course sold for $15.75, and basically it offered three systems: 1) The "hook system" (which, incidentally, "hooked" many), which begins by giving you a letter and a word for each number up to a hundred. 2) The second was the "chain method" where you need not memorize a whole speech but just a chain outline of key words. 3) The third was a "classification system" where you organized what you wanted to remember into categories of things with similarities.

In more recent years, much attention has been given to the artifical memory-code systems of associations. In 1976, thousands of people— ministers and laymen—flocked to seminars in Los Angeles and elsewhere, where they hoped to learn a simple system of memory by association. The "short cut" seekers were told that pictures are easier to remember than words. They were shown a series of cartoon images symbolizing phrases and concepts to be remembered. One example featured an illustration of a dove pulling a cross which stood on a loaf of bread that rested on an airplane; all this was held up by Satan with horns and forked tail and a stone in each upraised hand. This, if you please, is to help you fasten in your memory the exact words of Matthew 4:4—"Man shall not live by bread alone, but by every word that proceedeth out of the mouth of God."

Recently I received yet another large book on how to develop a fantastic "Bible Memory." It all boils down to "association" — logical or ridiculous — of the Bible verses to be learned with ideas and experiences already known. Because we have "grasshopper minds," the author says, the ideas already known will trigger the remembrance of the verses you wish to recall.

What are the conclusions regarding the use of the various memory improvement methods? *Mrs. Carlson* of Vicore's admitted that the artifical memory-code systems got in the way of natural learning and real comprehension. "The system involved not thinking, not reasoning," she said, "but pure and simple memory." *Dr. Ray Hyman*, Professor of Psychology at the University of Oregon, says of mnemonic systems, "They are not very useful except as parlor stunts (he used to be a magician). They've never been of any real practical help to me. I've found myself much better off not using them." Then he related a humorous *associational* dilemma which is not at all infrequent, "I've got a mental picture of one man I met who had a nose of an odd shape. I visualized it with water running over it. To this day, I can't recall if he is Mr. Brooks, Mr. Rivers or Mr. Trout!"

We know that realistic artwork does indeed illuminate a Scripture text for a child who cannot read. Simple associations may afford some memory help, particularly with respect to Bible references. Yet as a whole, we believe that the various memory improvement methods tend to obscure the meaning of the subject being learned and actually get in the way of natural memorization. Rather than taking time to learn and develop all the "associations," it is better just to learn the verses by natural concentration and enjoy the subject matter while you are doing it.

Strangely enough, *Mr. Lorayne* finally agreed that the extravagant memory methods were not profitable, when he said, "By using sneaky things in encouraging people to believe they can be mental wizards and getting them to concentrate on these methods, I am forcing them to do what they should do in the first place so they wouldn't need a memory system."

We come back therefore to the pure and simple conclusion that we assimilate the Word of God through the well-known mental exercise called *concentration*. You just cannot remember something unless you concentrate on it. You have to block everything else out of your mind and set your full attention on the Word of the

Lord. The mind either concentrates or wanders. Keeping the mind fixed on the sacred text pleases our God, who commands us to *lay up his words in our hearts* (Job. 22:22), and it honors the Holy Spirit whose mission it is to bring God's Word to our remembrance (Jn. 14:26). Recently, I came across an interesting testimony of a serviceman who wrote me about "the joy of learning the lessons each week." "However," he continued, "I must say that it was difficult at times to learn them. But if I would *concentrate* on what I was doing and followed the suggested plan of memorization, it was much easier than if I went about it half heartedly. Not only have I added more verses to my memory, but I also used the lessons and explanations for devotions in our church" (*Michael S. Nye*).

We do not mean to imply by all that has been said about mnemonics that we cannot improve the efficiency of our memory. Several fine suggestions are included in Chapter 4 — "Organization."

In learning the verses of Scripture, first ask the Lord to help you remember. Study the Scriptures in their Bible context and as you survey the verses, try to see how the verses form a definite connection with the topic heading.

"Whole learning" is generally considered more efficient than "part learning." Read through the entire assignment or chapter. After the framework of the Scripture passage has emerged, the details will fit in more meaningfully and more easily. You'll be remembering thoughts as well as words. Read it out loud several times. When you read silently, the picture is not clearly in view and your mind is more apt to wander. When you read it aloud, the picture becomes more vivid inasmuch as it is registering on the brain through the ear as well as through the eye. After the readings, try writing the verses. *Isaac Watts* observed that "once writing over what we desire to remember, and give due attention to what we write, will fix it more in mind than reading it five times."

The Four Rs of Memorization

Let me suggest four simple words (4 Rs!) which make up the vital framework of effective memorization:

REASON . . .

RECITATION . . .

RETROSPECTION . . .

RETENTION!

1) *Reason!* Why are you memorizing? What is your motive for doing it? Is it all that

important to you? Do you truly *desire* to do it? The problem in memorization is not generally one of *ability*, but of *desire*. Is this a settled issue between you and the Lord? If you truly desire to do it, then you have "stepped on the starter," and the engine of your brain is already running. *Motive* in *memorizing* is basic. Intention predisposes retention. This is the *reason* why you propose to spend time and mental resources, and your powers of concentration at once become tuned up and ready to assimilate: "Blessed are they which do hunger and thirst after righteousness: for they shall be filled" (Matt. 5:6).

2) *Recitation!* After you have learned the portion of Scripture, recite it out loud — either to yourself or, preferably to someone else. If it's not convenient to recite to someone else, a cassette recorder can serve as a Hearer. After reciting an assignment, you can play it back and find whether you memorized it *word perfect* and whether the expression with which you recited actually conveyed the meaning of the verse.

3) *Retrospection!* After you have recited the verses correctly a few times, turn your mind away completely to something else. Then after a significant time lapse, think back upon the verses and try reciting them again. Enjoying the verses in retrospection greatly strengthens your

memory efficiency. You are thus spacing out your concentration process which is a good phenomenon to put to use.

The mind is most receptive when there is at least outside interference. Better work is usually done in short periods, with lapses of time to help anchor the material in your memory.

"Over learn" the verses! This means put a little extra time on them after you already know them. This will prove of inestimable value and help to make your retrospection and review of the verses "*the joy and rejoicing of your heart*" (Jer. 15:16).

4) *Retention!* The object of all memorization is twofold: a) To enjoy and profit from the process of placing the holy Words of God into the storage bins of your brain. b) To have the verses permanently and instantly accessible for use in any opportunity and in every time of need. The memory retention will increase in proportion to the review of the verses, particularly a review in the actual use of those Scriptures.

"Gather my thoughts, good Lord,
they fitful roam
Like children bent on foolish wandering."

Learning to concentrate means acquiring a tremendous skill which will stand you in good stead no matter what is your vocation. Concentrating on God's Word will result in spiritual blessing and prosperity all the days of your life (Josh. 1:8). Young people who memorize prescribed portions of Scripture year after year generally discover that this becomes a great asset in high school and college, and the Word, readily accessible, makes their witness for the Lord spontaneous and effectual.

While we are on the subject of concentration, consider the exciting testimony of a young lad who lived in Great Britain almost 200 years ago. His name was Robert. In school he was called a *dunce* because it seemed he was too stupid to learn.

If Robert did not learn at school he learned at home. Every morning his father took down the big Bible and read it and prayed with his family. His mother loved the Scriptures, too. So many a day Robert sat with his Bible open committing to memory portions from its pages. Probably he often longed to shut the Book and run outside to join with his companions in their games. But his mother held him to the task. At twelve years of age he could recite the whole of Psalm 119. This is the longest chapter in the Bible.

98

One day the minister from the Presbyterian Church visited them. He had heard that Robert knew Psalm 119 by memory. "I would like to have him recite it in our church."

The next Sunday this twelve year old boy stood in front of the big congregation and recited perfectly the 119th Psalm. Believe it or not, from the time that Robert started to memorize Scripture he improved in his schoolwork.

Better still, while a boy he received into his heart Christ Jesus the Lord. He wrote out a pledge thus: "Jesus, I have given myself to Thy service. I learn from Thy Word that it is Thy holy pleasure that the gospel shall be preached to all nations. I desire to go where I am needed."

In the year 1807 he sailed for China, the very first Protestant missionary. In a letter to a friend he told how it was the memorizing of Scripture when he was a boy that influenced him to become a missionary.

He not only learned to speak their language like a Chinese person after a time, but he translated the Bible into that language, and wrote an English-Chinese dictionary in six large volumes.

Today, that boy who was known as a dunce is remembered as *Robert Morrison (1780-1831)*, who did a work for China that has probably never been equalled. And it all started with the memorization of Scripture!

Chapter Seven

ILLUMINATION . . . of the WORD

As we undertake to memorize the Word let us ask the Lord to enlighten our understanding:

"Open my eyes, that I may behold wondrous things out of Your law" (Ps. 119:18).

"The prayer implies a conscious darkness, a dimness of spiritual vision, a powerlessness to remove the defect, and full assurance that God can remove it. It shows also that the writer knew that there were vast treasures in the Word which he had not yet fully seen, marvels which he had not yet beheld, mysteries which he had scarcely believed. The Scriptures teem with marvels; *the*

Bible is wonder-land; it not only relates miracles, but it is itself a world of wonders. Yet what are these to closed eyes? And what man can open his own eyes, since he is born blind? God Himself must reveal truth to each heart. *Scripture needs opening, but not one half so much as our eyes do; the veil is not on the book,* but on our hearts. What perfect precepts, what precious promises, what priceless privileges are neglected by us because we wander among them like blind men among the beauties of nature, and they are to us as a landscape shrouded in darkness!

"The Psalmist had a measure of spiritual perception, or he would never have known that there were wondrous things to be seen, nor would he have prayed, 'open my eyes'; but what he had seen made him long for a clearer and wider sight" (*C. H. Spurgeon*).

Our determination and ability to memorize the Word of our heavenly Father increases in proportion to our spiritual perception and appreciation of it.

"Open my eyes, that I may see,
Glimpses of truth you have for me;
Place in my hands the wonderful key
That shall unclasp, and set me free.
Silently now I wait for Thee,

Ready, my Lord, Your will to see;
Open my eyes, illumine me, Spirit, divine!"
— *Chas. H. Scott*

The memorization of the Word, however diligently undertaken, will be sterile and barren if it is unenlightened and uninspired by the Holy Spirit.

Memorizing the Word of God at once becomes easier and more profitable when the meaning of it is understood. There is not much immediate value in learning something which you do not comprehend. Basically, the *illumination* of the human mind with respect to the Holy Scriptures involves the ministry of the Holy Spirit who enables a person to understand and to appropriate them.

In the process of enlightenment the divine Teacher uses various means which we are to observe. These certainly include careful *reading* of the particular Scripture (1 Tim. 4:13), diligent *study* (2 Tim. 2:15), *searching* of the text (Jn. 5:39) and *comparing* the different portions of God's revelation which bear upon the subject (1 Cor. 2:13).

One of the most concise, yet complete statements dealing with understanding divine truth is found in *Myles Coverdale's Rules for*

Reading the Bible (1535). In his prologue to the reader, he wrote,

> "It shall greatly help ye
> to understande Scripture,
> if thou mark not only
> what is spoken or wrytten,
> but of whom and to whom,
> with what words,
> at what time, where,
> to what intent,
> with what circumstances,
> considering what goeth before
> and what followeth."

What is written? In order to understand Scripture, it is necessary to get at the real substance of *what* is written. What is God actually telling us in the particular verses?

Of Whom? When Philip recognized that the Ethiopian eunuch was reading the prophecy of Isaiah, he said to him, "Do you understand what you are reading?" (Acts 8:30). Among other things, the devout Ethiopian asked, "Of whom speaks the prophet thus?" Philip "began at the same Scripture" (Isa. 53:7, 8), "and preached unto him Jesus" (Acts 8:35). In one way or another, all of Scripture relates to the Lord Jesus Christ.

104

To whom? We need always to give due consideration *to whom* a passage was primarily written. The Scripture divides all mankind into three general categories: the Jew, the Gentile and the Church (1 Cor. 10:32). We must distinguish between things that differ, but as Christians, not do so at the expense of taking over all blessings in the Bible intended for the children of Israel and leave for the poor sons of Abraham all the curses.

With what words? Divine inspiration of the Bible extends to every word that has been given; this is why we need to analyze it word by word and ponder upon the exact meaning of each word. Although the rhythmic dignity and cadence of the King James version will probably never be superseded, it is good to consult other reliable translations in order to fathom the full meaning of the text. Commentaries, concordance, word study books and other reference works generally prove helpful.

At what time? It is important to note when a particular Book of the Bible was written. For example, some parts of the New Testament were written after the fall of Jerusalem in A. D. 70, and so the teaching in those Scriptures on eschatology (doctrine of the last things) cannot refer to the destruction of the Holy City.

Where? When you consider where Paul was when he wrote Philippians, you cannot help but be amazed that this epistle—whose keynote is *joy*—came out of that damp and dirty underground dungeon in Rome.

Under what circumstances? 1 Thessalonians was written to instruct and comfort the Christians there who were looking for the immediate return of the Lord, and were confused by the fact that some of their number had died (1 Thess. 4:13-18).

To what intent? How often we have heard John 15:6 used in discussion on the final preservation of the saints, the exercise of free-will and other related questions. But when you find out that the whole paragraph (Jn. 15:1-6) is a discourse on fruit-bearing and not salvation, all the controversy quickly disappears.

The context? In order to understand Scripture, it is exceedingly needful to study it in its context and consider carefully "what goes before" and "what follows after."

These are some of the basic principles of Bible study that need always to be observed until the portion of the Word is so clearly illuminated that, at the very mention of the reference, the truth leaps into view.

In preparing the Scripture Memory Books described in Chapter Four, much effort was expended in providing various helps for understanding the Scriptures. The difficult words were defined and ample notes were included with the verses, always bearing in mind the age-level of the participants in the different Memory Books.

It is well to keep in mind that children will always remember it better when the subject matter tends to capture their imagination. Vivid colors and realistic drawings which are designed to illustrate the truth of Scripture are of immense value.

A few pertinent lines from *Horace* on the subject:

"Sounds which address the ear are lost and die
In one short hour; but that which strikes the eye,
Lives long upon the mind; the faithful sight
Engraves the knowledge with a beam of light."

Much care must be used, however, to make certain that the drawings do indeed illuminate the text. Artwork may be very impressive but serves only to distract and confuse the young impressionable minds. The use of abstract art and drawings which merely satisfy the aesthetic senses and do not aid in understanding the Scriptures may prove to be a hindrance in that they tend to immerse the mind in corporeal images and render the child's mind unfit to take in intellectual ideas, or cause him to form wrong conceptions of spiritual things.

The main purpose of drawings, illustrations and other helps should always be to facilitate the understanding of the truth, particularly for children.

Young Children Memorizing Scripture

Indeed, there are certain "authorities" in our day, as there have been probably in every age, who tell us that memorizing Scripture is not desirable for children because the truth is not understood and is not related to the child's experience. But the *authority* of the Scriptures contradicts such ideas. Through *Moses*, God said, "These words which I command you this day, shall be in your heart. And you shall teach them diligently unto your children, and shall talk of them when you sit in your house, and when you walk by the way, and when you lie down, and when you rise up" (Deut. 6:6, 7).

We have the revealing instruction in Isaiah which tells us that doctrine and Scripture are to be the diet even of babes: "Whom shall he teach knowledge? And whom shall he make to understand doctrine? Them that are weaned from the milk, and drawn from the breasts. For precept must be upon precept, precept upon precept; line upon line, line upon line; here a little, and there a little" (Isa. 28:9, 10).

Little by little, impressions are made by the Word of God in the experience of children, "as the Spirit opens their understanding." First comes the light for the new birth and then more light for growth into spiritual character and service. The days and nights, the months, the seasons come and go, and during all that time there continues the learning, the remembering, the reciting, the repeating of the Words of the Spirit, growing thereby, and going to worship and serving the Lord.

The Apostle Paul commended Timothy's mother, Eunice, and his grandmother, Lois, for their part in encouraging Timothy to "lay up" the Word of God in his mind and heart from the time he was an infant (2 Tim. 3:14, 15).

If difficulties arise in the process due to the child's immaturity and levity of mind, they are more than balanced by the child's freedom from the prejudices of older folk, and the perplexing cares of life that hinder the adult from taking in God's Word. Little children instinctively desire to penetrate the unknown; they seize upon explanations of nature and of God with eagerness; they accept the revelation of God and the explanation of their teacher with unsuspecting confidence.

If objections are raised that children cannot grasp the meaning of Scripture, it is well to remember that actually man, at no stage of life, can comprehend the things of God (1 Cor. 2:14). At every level of human experience it takes the work of the Holy Spirit to learn spiritual truth and "to know the things that are freely given to us of God" (1 Cor. 2:12). The Bible is a closed book to the unregenerate person. He cannot see anything interesting in it because he is blind; but when the Spirit touches the scales of the eyes, they fall off; and when He applies the salve, the eyes of his spiritual understanding are enlightened (Eph. 1:18) and the words of truth become personally relevant and precious.

The Holy Spirit indwells the believer the moment he is saved (1 Cor. 6:19). This means that the most distinguished private Tutor takes up residence in each believer (1 Jn. 2:27); Who "will guide you into all truth" (Jn. 16:13). He will unlock and unfold the sacred mysteries of God, "yea, the deep things of God" (1 Cor. 2:10). He has intimate knowledge of *all* things, *all* truth, *all* events, *all* beings. He delights to open our understanding that we might more fully know and glorify our Lord Jesus Christ (Jn. 16:13, 14).

The Word of God is a "critic" of the thoughts and intentions of the heart (Heb. 4:12), and as we assimilate it into our heads and submit to its authority, the Holy Spirit works it into our hearts and takes us *inside*, as it were, and opens our eyes to see "wondrous things" out of His law.

In our attempts to search for and understand the truth, we may read commentaries, listen to other brethren expound the truth; but in all seeking, we must ever have that abiding conviction that our real Teacher is the Holy Spirit. Unless He has "opened our understanding," unless He has instructed us, we have not really been taught.

John Chrysostom (345-407) advised a young friend who said he could not understand the Bible, as follows: "Take the Bible in your hands. Read the whole story, and bearing in mind the things which are clear, pursue again and again those which are dark and difficult. And if after frequent reading ye find not the sense of a passage go to a brother more learned than yourself. And should no man open to you that which you seek, God Himself will surely reveal it unto you."

Chapter Eight

RELAXATION . . .with the WORD

Several years ago, in Memphis, Tennessee, at the conclusion of a service, a man came up to talk with me about his frustrations in trying to memorize Scripture. "I belieEe God wants me to memorize His Word," he said, "and I see the need for it in my life, but I just cannot do it; if I continue in this way I'm afraid I'll have a nervous breakdown." As the dear brother unburdened his problem to me, he became progressively more agitated at the very thought of his predicament. Then he stopped abruptly and turned to me with this question, "Do you have any suggestions which might help me memorize the Scriptures?"

"Yes indeed," I replied, "relax. . . . enjoy it. . . . you have nothing better to do."

The brother in Memphis is certainly not the only one who has struggled with this matter. It's a strange thing that although children do not generally understand the Scriptures as well and do not possess the same degree of appreciation for the Word, yet they memorize faster and remember longer than the average adult. The great hymn writer, *Isaac Watts*, in his long essay, "The Improvement of the Mind" attempts to explain the causes underlying this phenomenon.

"In old age, men have a very feeble remembrance of things that were done of late, that is, the same day or week or year; the brain has grown so hard, that the present images or strokes make little or no impression, and therefore they immediately vanish. . . ."

Watts states further that as we get older the brain shrinks and hardens from lack of use, and that the best therapy for the brain is memorizing, and of course the best thing to memorize is Scripture.

Pressures that Hinder Memorizing

What is it really that keeps adults from memorizing the Word? I have heard many people tell me their reasons, or, perhaps more accurately, their excuses; these can be reduced to three or four kinds of built-in defenses:

1) *The pressure of time.* Over and over again people say: "I just don't have time to do it." There is no denying the fact that we all seem always to be pushed with more things to do than we have time. But as you reflect upon this dilemma, is it not generally true that we manage to find time for those things that we really desire to do most? It's a matter of setting up the right priorities. Furthermore we are specifically instructed, "See then that you walk circumspectly, not as fools, but as wise, redeeming the time, because the days are evil" (Eph. 5:16, 17).

Often the plea of insufficient time is advanced by pastors and other Christian workers. It is primarily to all of us who are in the Lord's work that *Dr. Webb Garrison* directed his pungent remarks several years ago, "Dare I say it?" he began, "I wonder whether perhaps more of the Lord's work would be done if Christian leaders (paid and volunteer) would divert half an hour a day from activities that produce results on the statistical tables and zealously spend it memorizing and repeating Scripture."

2) *The pressure of earning a living*; school, washing dishes and other "cares of this life" seem always to assert themselves convincingly against spiritual pursuits. There is no question but that we have to take care of these legitimate responsibilities, but here we must not forget the words of our Lord — "Take no thought for your life, what you shall eat, or what you shall drink; nor yet for your body, what you shall put on. Is not the life more than meat and the body than raiment? . . . (For after all these things do the Gentiles seek:) for your heavenly Father knows that you have need of all these things. But seek you first the kingdom of God, and His righteousness; and all these things shall be added unto you" (Matt. 6:25, 32, 33).

Earning a living is necessary, but God would have us know "that man does not live by bread only, but by every word that proceeds out of the mouth of the Lord does man live" (Deut. 8:3). It is very easy in our fast-moving society to feast the body and famish the soul. We lose appetite for the Word, spiritual anemia sets in; and although we may have Bibles on every hand, we become overtaken by the "famine . . . of hearing the words of the Lord" (Amos 8:11).

116

3) *Then there is that pressure* which comes
from an erroneous conclusion that is so frequently sounded: "I just cannot memorize!"
Unquestionably, there are a few people around
who may find it quite impossible to memorize.
But by far and large we can all memorize God's
Word if we really desire to do it.

First, ask the Lord to help you. He will
indeed help because He has instructed and
commanded us to do it (Deut. 6:6-8; 11:18; Job
22:22). Without Him we "can do nothing" (Jn.
15:5), but as we draw closer to our Lord and
allow His strength and wisdom to become our
portion, we will be amazed at His enabling
grace, and we shall confidently exclaim with
the Apostle, "I can do all things through Christ
who strengthens me" (Phil. 4:13).

4) *The feeling of disappointment* at not being able to remember and recall all the verses
memorized after an interval of time *exerts its
own peculiar pressure on every one of us.*

First, let us be reminded that the only
way anybody can possibly recall the Scriptures
memorized for any length of time is by constant use of those verses and by an intelligent
review of them, in a systematic way. Reciting
them out loud to someone else at home, school

or at work helps tremendously to seal them in your mind.

Second, we must not allow ourselves to think that the verses memorized are *all* forgotten. We never quite forget all the verses that have been memorized. When you hear a preacher using one of those Scriptures you thought had eluded you completely, it is interesting how much more meaningful it is, and you recognize the verse at least in part. The same thing is true when you come across verses you've memorized in your Bible reading. If you give attention to memorizing God's Word, the Holy Spirit will bring it to your remembrance in time of need (Jn. 14:26) and He will bless your heart with truths which you were possibly not in the habit of recalling. But He certainly cannot bring it to remembrance if you have not taken the time to put it in your mind.

But supposing you did forget every verse you've memorized; there is still immense value because of the blessing received in the very process of memorization. I read about the man who complained to his pastor that he was much discouraged from memorizing the Scriptures in that he could not fasten anything in his memory that would remain.

The elderly pastor had him take a pitcher, and fill it with water. When he had done it, he bade him empty it completely and wipe it clean so that nothing should remain of it. At that point the man wondered what was the meaning of it. "Now," said the pastor, "though there be nothing of the water remaining in it, yet the pitcher is cleaner than it was before. So, though your memory may seemingly retain nothing of the Word you memorize, yet your heart is cleaner because the Word went through it."

About 20 years ago or so, a lady came to me after a service in East Texas and said, "I simply cannot remember anything, because my mind is like a sieve; the Word just runs through." "Keep memorizing the Word, Sister," I said, "it will keep your mind clean while it's running through."

But let's get back to Mr. "Memphis" who was so greatly disturbed because he could not *hold* the Word of God in his memory! We have to admit that the cares of this life have a way of constantly asserting themselves and demanding first and immediate attention from us every day. We are so much in the habit of thinking that those are the things that we just *have* to do right now or else all of life will collapse. But is this really true? Is this what God desires for us?

Nothing More Important to Do

A number of years ago, the Lord showed me very clearly that being occupied with Him over the Word was the most important part of my life. Then it occurred to me that I did not have to be concerned about how long it took to memorize a certain passage of Scripture because I really did not have anything more important to do! This helped me in memorizing God's Word more than anything else. It does not matter how long it takes. Just relax and relish the sweetness of the Word as you joyfully try to place the very words of God into the memory chambers of your mind.

Think about the meaning of it! Consider each word, each phrase, each sentence. Say it out loud; say it to yourself or to others; say it with expression and conviction. This is indeed the Word of God, and you are attaching great significance to it and putting it into that long term level area of your mind.

Recognize that Satan is at work in this area and he will do everything in his power to pressure you with the cares of this life. This is a spiritual battle; resist Satan and his attempts to rush you and crowd you with the many responsibilities of this life (Phil. 4:6).

God is sovereign; He knows what you need; He loves you most dearly. He cares for you. Believe it and ask Him to help you assimilate the precious words of life. Don't let the busyness of this life keep you from receiving the nourishment and blessedness that God has for you in His Word.

"Where the word of a king is, there is power" (Ecc. 8:4). As the Word of the Lord is in the heart, "there is power" against sin, there is power against anxiety, there is power against the manifold trials that come our way. Satan knows that he will be defeated in your life in proportion to the way you allow the Word to "dwell richly" in your heart (Col. 3:16).

The mind that is at rest and free from the assaulting pressures of this life will absorb the Word of God like a sponge. I often think of how restful and relaxing the Word of God can be.

Thirsting for the Lord

In this regard, let's just take a brief look at Psalm 63.

The Psalmist *awakens*, and at once thirsts for a renewed sense of the Lord's presence (Ps. 63:1, 2): "O God, You art my God; early will I seek You: my soul thirsts for You, my flesh longs for You in a dry and thirsty land, where no water is; to see Your power and Your glory, so as I have seen You in the sanctuary." It is quite obvious that this man is occupied — mind, soul and spirit — with the presence of the Lord and not with the schedule that lies ahead of him for that day.

In the next verses of Psalm 63 (3-5), there is an expression of grateful praise: "Because Your lovingkindness is better than life; my lips shall praise You. Thus will I bless You while I live: I will lift up my hands in Your name. My soul shall be satisfied as with marrow and fatness; and my mouth shall praise You with joyful lips."

The thought of the Lord's presence and the Lord's lovingkindness is regarded as *better than life*." The day seems to have passed quickly as the pilgrim was occupied with the Lord and all through the day His soul followed hard after him (vs. 8).

In the *evening* he recalls God's mercies (Ps. 63:6-8): "When I remember You upon my bed, and meditate on You in the night watches. Because You have been my help, therefore in the shadow of Your wings will I rejoice. My soul follows hard after You: Your right hand upholds

122

me." He praises the Lord for what God is to him; for the Lord's help; he rejoices in the Lord's protection and the fact that it is God's right hand that upholds him.

Enjoying the Lord and His Bounty

Now relax on the hillside with David and let your soul delight in fatness as you slowly ponder the varied ramifications of life touched upon in this familiar Psalm 23. You must not rush. It shrivels into nothing if you hurry over it.

First there is the Lord's provision (Ps. 23:1, 2): The shepherd is none other than God Himself and the sheep is none other than you or me. "The Lord is my shepherd; I shall not want. He makes me to lie down in green pastures: He leads me beside the still waters." Once I was weary and hungry and now I dwell in the pastures of His provision in quietness and peace.

Next there is the Lord's protection (Ps. 23:3, 4): "He restores my soul: He leads me in the path of righteousness for His name's sake. Yea, though I walk through the valley of the shadow of death, I will fear no evil: for You are with me; Your rod and staff they comfort me." He restores my soul and He leads me in the paths of righteousness for His own name's sake. Often the way is dangerous and dark, but He knows the way inasmuch as He has trod it alone, and so I follow Him down to the deep gorges, along the rocky ledges and into the swollen streams unafraid because, *"You are with me."*

And then there is communion with the Lord (Ps. 23:5, 6): "You prepare a table before me in the presence of my enemies: You anoint my head with oil; my cup runs over. Surely goodness and mercy shall follow me all the days of my life: and I will dwell in the house of the Lord forever." The journey is nearly ended and the shining mansions are in view. The enemies who have pursued will molest me no more. The heavenly footmen will follow me all the days of my life; they are really the Lord Himself bearing the names of "goodness" and "mercy."

Hallelujah! "My cup runs over," and "I shall dwell in the house of the Lord forever."

Now, why should anyone feel compelled to rush in memorizing such precious words that so revealingly and beautifully tell of our wonderful Lord and our close relationship with Him?

Realizing the fact that meditating on the Word and memorizing it was the first business of the day for me and that I had nothing more important to do—just this realization—has

124

helped me to assimilate God's Word more readily than anything else I've tried. It works. It will work for anybody. It doesn't really matter how long it takes you to do it. *You don't have anything better to do – do you?*

You will find that your ability to memorize and remember will improve as you go along. This is the testimony of every person—young and older. This is what *Isaac Watts* means when he says, "Our memories will be in a great measure molded and formed, improved or injured, according to the exercise of them. If you never use them they will be almost lost. Those who are wont to converse or read about a few things only will retain but a few in their memory. Those who are used to remember things but for an hour, and charge their memories with it no longer, will retain them but an hour before they vanish."

Now the matter of forgetting is not all bad. The art of memorizing involves the power to forget some things. This may seem contradictory but it's true. There are many things that God wants us to "forget" (Phil. 3:13). We must not allow our minds to be tormented by past failures or sins, which God has forgiven and removed from us as far as the "east is from the west." We must forget them. Furthermore we must not allow our minds to be cluttered with worthless slogans, stories, chit-chat and profitless accumulations of mere trash. Therefore, the ability to forget should not always be regarded as a weakness. Thank God that we can forget some things!

Suppose that you have been able to purchase a very expensive golden chest, which obviously cost a large sum of money; everybody that sees it marvels not only at such a possession but, much more, they are intrigued with much curiosity as to what such a rare encasement would contain. They suspect all sorts of things, and can hardly wait to see what you have in it. Then, imagine their sense of disappointment when the chest is opened and they notice that you have in it pieces of string, rubber bands, paper clips, laundry claim checks, parking tickets, buttons, used tea bags, etc., etc.!

What a disappointment and what a shame to have such a valuable chest all lined in beautiful velvet and used for collecting bits of trash.

That golden chest, friend, is really the brain which God has given to each one of us; as God sees it, and if it could be opened for others to behold its contents, what would they see? We know what it is that God would have us to store in that "golden chest" called the brain. Unquestionably, He would desire for it to be filled with the treasure of His own wonderful Word. "This most precious jewel is to be preferred above all treasure. If thou be hungry, it is meat to satisfy thee; if thou be thirsty, it is drink to refresh thee; if thou be sick, it is a pleasant remedy; if thou be weak, it is a staff to lean upon; if thine enemy assault thee; it is a sword to fight with withal if thou be in darkness, it is a lantern to guide thy feet; if thou be doubtful of the way, it is a bright shining star to direct thee; if thou be in displeasure with God, it is the message of reconciliation; if thou study to save the soul, receive the engrafted Word, for that is able to do it: it is the Word of life" (*Edwin Sandys*, 1519-1587).

Dr. Wilfred T. Grenfell, (1865-1940), once a missionary in Labrador, gave witness to the value of having the Word of God treasured up in our minds for every possible need. He said many years ago:

"Most gladly I give the testimony of my experience concerning the memorizing of Scripture. To me it has been an unfailing help in doubt, anxiety, sorrow, and all the countless vicissitudes and problems of life. I believe in it enough to have devoted many, many hours to stowing away passages where I can neither leave them behind me nor be unable to get at them. Facing death alone while stranded on a floating section of ice on a partially frozen ocean, the comradeship it afforded me supplied all I needed. With my whole soul I commend to others the giving of some little time each day to secure the immense returns Scripture memorization insures."

Chapter Nine

MEDITATION . . . in the WORD

Memorization of God's precepts makes *meditation* possible day and night, and in turn, *meditation* facilitates a better understanding and sinks the roots of Holy Writ more deeply into memory's recesses. Memorization and meditation always go together. They are not synonymous in meaning, but they are absolutely inseparable. Memorizing Scripture without the valuable exercise of meditation is like eating food without the process of digestion. The great Book of Psalms opens with that concept: "But his delight is in the law of the Lord and in His law doth he meditate day and night" (Ps. 1:2). Enjoying the Word and delighting in it inevitably results in a spiritual exercise of communion with God.

Two Hebrew words (*Hagah* and *Siach*), similar in meaning, are used some 38 times in the Psalter to convey the thought of meditation. They do not carry just the meaning of thinking and reflecting, but they carry the ideas of talking, uttering, murmuring, speaking, complaining, conversing, communing, declaring, praying and praising. Meditation is a devotional exercise where a person engages in framing his thoughts in words and expressing them either to himself, to others, or to God.

Marie Harrington, from Texas, whom we had the joy of encouraging to memorize the Word, found out quickly the need for meditation. She wrote:

> "Scriptures are not meant to be swallowed whole, they are meant for deep meditation; brought back to mind and thought on again for periods of long duration."

What is Meditation

Meditation is a process of prayerful and personal reflection—a concentrated and unhurried thought—upon the meaning of the Word.

Devout meditation is a prolonged exercise of infusing every area of life with the divine Word. The whole nature will become immersed in the Scriptures till they penetrate the whole being; the mind becomes saturated with holy thoughts, the heart is motivated with holy affections and the memory is filled with holy associations. And we may be very certain that every time the remembrance of the Lord's Word crosses our minds it is the Holy Spirit's fulfillment of our Lord's promise that, "He shall teach you all things, and bring all things to your remembrance, whatsoever I have said unto you" (Jn. 14:26b).

"Scriptures are stored in our memories
And the Spirit makes application;
In times of need, He helps us recall
And see their proper relation."
— M. Harrington

God is able to reveal to our hearts the deeper meanings as we spend time pondering over the Word. Several years ago, a friend from West Virginia made this discovery. "How great a blessing your memory plan has been to me," she said, "I never cease to be amazed at how often the topic and verses seem to be exactly what I needed that very week! It's also amazing how as you go over and over the words, deeper meanings and insights just sort of unfold. I don't retain the verses as well as I would like, but it would be worth taking a course just for the blessing it gives as the verses are meditated on, even if I couldn't remember any of them a year later" (*Mrs. R. G. Kelso*).

After concentrating on the Word, whether in study or memorization, let us take care not to plunge ourselves immediately thereafter into some amusements or other activities which Satan is so eager to use in an attempt to reduce or nullify the blessing of the Word. Let us take time to recollect and repeat the things that have been learned. Share them with others if possible. At all costs, do not allow the rich treasures of God's Word to be washed away from your mind by a torrent of other activities, nor let them become crowded out by the demands of other situations.

Is not this the meaning of that "good ground," where "in an honest and good heart, having heard the Word" they "keep it" (Lu. 8:15)? The word *katecho* means "to keep in memory," as it is rendered in 1 Corinthians 15:2. Satan knows how potent God's Word is and how it produces spiritual results if allowed to take root in the good soil of the mind and heart. He resorts to many expedients in an effort to distract and remove God's Word from the mind. He will remind us about the cares of this life; he will get us all wrought up regarding the deceitfulness of riches, and the pleasures of this life. Our Lord emphasized how imperative it is for the believer *to keep the Word in memory*, to think on it, to meditate upon it, hold it fast, and allow it to "bring forth fruit with patience" (Lu. 8:15).

Meditation upon the memorized Scripture is probably the believer's most profitable occupation; without the Word, the so-called meditation quickly degenerates at best into a profitless daydreaming or it becomes a time of dwelling upon our disappointments and other unhallowed recollections.

The Psalmist rose to the heights of heavenly contemplation when he exclaimed, "Oh how love I Thy law; it is my meditation all the day. . . ." He was aware of how God ministered to him through the Word, which grows into his life, his attitudes, and his actions. It made him "wiser" and "more understanding." It kept him from "every evil way," and enabled him to discern the "false teachings." Meditating in the Word only increased his appetite for it the more, as he himself testified, "How sweet are Thy words unto my taste! Yea, sweeter than honey to my mouth" (Ps. 119:97-104). Such a relish for the Word will cause *soul-rise* before *sunrise* as in Psalm 119:147—"Early, even before the dawning of the morning, did I make supplication: I hoped in Thy Word" (*Delitzsch*). This is God's plan! Read and memorize the Word by day, and in the night watches, when sleep eludes you, muse upon it. Yes, in the day of prosperity we may sing the Psalms (God's hymn book), and in the time of affliction we may comfort ourselves with promises out of the same Book.

God's Word Distills as the Dew

In the night seasons—in those times of dryness and desolation—God's Word silently falls on our souls to revive and to prepare us for the trials of the day. "My speech shall distill as the dew," God says, "as the small rain on the tender herb. . . ." (Deut. 32:2). Just as the tiny dewdrops revive the little stems of the fading plants with the life-renewing moisture, so God keeps on distilling His "speech"—His precious nutriment—into our frail spiritual life, or it would soon wither during the seasons of fiery trials and burning heat. Our minds never sleep and it's truly amazing how God refreshes our

134

spirits during the hours of sleep when, it seems, the Word which we have assimilated previously nourishes our hearts and minds. We do not hear any sound of abundance of rain; our senses are not aroused; we may be too sick or too wearied from battle and unable to *take in* any words; but just the same, midst the spiritual desolation, or the wilderness journey, God tenderly watches over us and His Word—His comforting, His enlivening "speech" — keeps on distilling softly as the dew, "and thereby strengthening our hearts and minds through Christ Jesus."

"Springs of life on desert places
Shalt thy God unseal for thee;
Quickening and reviving graces,
Dew-like, healing, sweet and free."

How blessed these truths have been to me during many nights of indescribable anguish and trial! Fighting high fever and weird hallucinations, I could almost feel His gentle footsteps near me! Perhaps this is what the Psalmist was going through when he said, "When I remember Thee upon my bed, and meditate on Thee in the night watches" (63:6).

Memory has a way of getting very busy while we are waiting for sleep that seems slow in coming, and never perhaps are we more tempted to useless recollections and fearful speculations. We have all struggled against those superhuman powers which seemed to close in on us with cruel threatenings! Then the "small rain" of the Word begins gently to fall — "Now" — not last week — but "now" — not tomorrow, but "now" — right "now" — "the God of hope (God never gives up hope concerning a single one of His children) fill you with all joy and peace in believing..." (Rom. 15:13). Blessed be God! Things are not *hopeless* — they are *hope-filled*! This is indeed the very help in time of need and the bright hope amidst the blackest darkness! This night let us "remember" Him and *"meditate on"* Him *"in the night watches!"*

We can only recall and meditate thus on what we already know! Thanks be to God that we have that God-given, solid and abiding Word of the Lord for our memory!

"My meditation of Him shall be sweet:
I will be glad in the Lord" (Ps. 104:34).

"I will sing unto the Lord as long as I live:
I will sing praise to my God
while I have my being" (Ps. 104:33).

On one such night I awakened out of a sound sleep singing out loud one of *Ackley's* lovely hymns which I hadn't thought of in many years:

"Within my heart I hold a fadeless memory, The dearest memory I know, The memory of One who died on Calvary, whose heart was broken for my sin and woe.

"Memory! Memory! Blessed memory that leads me back to Calvary, when I was lost the Savior found me, Put His loving arms around me, That's a memory that never fades."

I know what some of you are thinking right now! This is all well and good, but I can hardly find time to read or memorize the Scriptures, much less taking time for meditation on it!

*Dear friend—young or older—*and whoever you are, you simply must *take time!* You must, or you will most certainly be fading away.

The Apostle Paul was a very, very busy pioneering missionary and preacher! Agreed? Well, we find in Acts 20:13, 14 that his missionary companions sailed from Taos to Assos, but Paul "minding himself to go on foot" that ten or fifteen miles! Why did he do such a thing? Was he tired of his fellow-laborers? No! I am confident that Paul felt the great need of being alone with the Lord and he planned that solitary walk for the specific purpose of prayer, meditation and quiet communion with the Lord!

Of all the people, the Lord's servants must at all cost somehow find time to assimilate God's word, to meditate on it day and night and by means of it commune alone with the Lord, or else they will become mere religious propagandists and their words will be but a sounding brass and tinkling cymbals (1 Cor. 13:1).

The Blessings of Meditation

It seems to me nothing is more urgently *essential* to a continuing and profitable Scripture memorization than *meditation* — Spirit-guided meditation upon the Spirit-inspired Word!

Why is meditation on the memorized Word so absolutely essential?

Consider thoughtfully the summarization of what we have been trying to say in this chapter:

1) It is through *meditation* that we sink the Word more deeply into our memory!

2) It is through *meditation* that we come to understand the Scripture better and draw out the deep truths which before seem to lie concealed in darkness.

138

3) It is by *meditation* that we draw out various inferences and establish in our minds spiritual principles relating to Bible knowledge.

4) It is by *meditation* upon the Word that we are enabled to evaluate what we read and what we hear and by the illumination of the Holy Spirit, distinguish between truth and error.

5) *Meditation* in the Word is the surest way of meeting with the Lord in sweet communion.

Dr. J. R. Miller, who wrote several excellent devotional books a few decades ago, said, "The *very best thing* we can do for people in this world of sin and sorrow is to get the Words of Christ into their hearts. The living Christ walks among the glades of God's Word and we meet Him there in sweet communion as we meditate therein day and night! 'O how love I Thy law.' "

6) *Meditation* upon the Word soon turns to communion and then to fervent prayer where we use the inspired promises and praises in our intercessions and thanksgivings. It must delight the heart of our heavenly Father as we express to Him the very words He gave us, just as it thrills a parent to hear his child repeating the words which he learned from the parent and now remembers them and speaks them with personal conviction.

George Mueller discovered after a good many years of serving the Lord that instead of beginning his day with prayer, it was much more profitable "to begin to meditate on the Word of God, searching as it were into every verse to get the blessing out of it . . . in order to obtain food for my soul . . . so that, though I did not as it were, give myself to prayer, but to meditation, yet it turned almost immediately more or less into prayer. Food for my soul is the object of my meditation. The result of this is that there is always a good deal of confession, thanksgiving, supplication, or intercession mingled with my meditation." This is a vital point.

7) Memorizing Scripture and *meditating* upon it thoughtfully brings new and thrilling insights; freguently, it is a whole set of fresh ideas that bless the heart.

8) At other times, Scriptures which have been brought together into the mind, through memorization and *meditation*, instead of being scattered in various Books of the Bible, have a way of forming an unexpected cohesion and producing a new insight into the wonderful Word of God.

Great spiritual objectives are suggested by two words: "meditation" and "delight." "I will

140

meditate in thy precepts, and have respect unto
Thy law. I will delight myself in Thy statutes: I
will not forget Thy law" (Ps. 119:15, 16).

In our day of much activity and much
going to and fro, *meditation* seems to have become a lost art. We do not strive to improve the
capacity for sustained thought on a given subject, nor are we eager to engage in a prolonged,
quiet consideration of the Word of truth. This
represents an area of great spiritual need. May
those of us who have memorized God's Word
go a step further and reap the wonderful benefits that God has for those who take time
with His Word. Can we say with real heart
conviction?

"I will meditate in Thy precepts . . ."
"I will delight myself in Thy statutes."

May the life of each one of us be charac-
terized by a more habitual *meditation* upon the
Scriptures. It is not the splash of diving into the
sea, but actually staying there a while that results in the gathering of a good quantity of
pearls. Let us purpose in our hearts to meditate
upon the Word of God, to draw out from it the
nutriment, the encouragement, the wisdom, the
strength, and the blessing that God has there for
us from day to day.

Take for example the first verse of Psalm 103, which is said to be the very center of the Old Testament. *A. B. Simpson* called those first verses the true pivot on which to hang our faith, our hope, our happiness and our holiness: "Bless the Lord, O my soul, and all that is within me, bless His holy name. Bless the Lord, O my soul, and forget not all His benefits" (Ps. 103:1, 2).

The Lord and His benefits are inseparable. He Himself is our all in all — and with Him God has freely given us all things (Rom. 8:32).

Some of those wonderful benefits from the Lord are gratefully enumerated in the first verses of Psalm 103:

1) *Release*: "who forgiveth all thine iniquities."

2) *Restoration*: "who healeth all thy diseases.

3) *Redemption*: "who redeemeth thy life from destruction."

4) *Resources*: "who crowneth thee with lovingkindness and tender mercies."

5) *Refreshing*: "who satisfieth thy mouth with good things."

6) *Renewal*: "So that thy youth is renewed like the eagles."

Amen and amen and amen!

"Bless the Lord, ye His angels,
that excel in strength,
that do His commandments,
hearkening unto the voice of His word.

"Bless the Lord, all ye His hosts;
ye ministers of His, that do His pleasure.

"Bless the Lord, all His works
in all places of His dominion:

"Bless the Lord, O my soul"
(Ps. 103:20-22).

Chapter Ten

APPROPRIATION ... of the WORD

There is something to be said for memorizing Scriptures just for the sake of memorizing—storing them away for future use—but it is much better if the Scriptures provide meaning and help at the present as well as at some future date. The real test of Scriptures "learned" lies not in the ability to recite them word for word but in the understanding and the application of the truth to the daily life.

Memorizing and meditating on the

Scriptures is not just an idle comtemplation — a wasteful loitering around the throne of grace — it must be with the view of *obedience* and *submission* to God's Word: "Thou shalt meditate in the book of the law day and night, that thou mayest observe to do according to all that is written therein" (Josh. 1:8). It is encouraging to see that so many of the folk who are memorizing the Word systematically are actually using it in their daily lives.

From Fairbanks, Alaska, *Miss Debbie Henry* writes: "I enjoy learning the verses, and they greatly help me in my spiritual life. It is thrilling to me to be able to witness to a friend with some verses I learned the previous week." And then I see a heartwarming testimony from *Mrs. Shirley McCartney*, Edmond, Oklahoma, who has been seriously ill for so long and who writes as follows: "I thank the Lord often for the Bible verses that I have committed to memory and I know I never would have done it if it had not been for this system. It seems that when I am the lowest He preaches me one of His sermonettes through the precious Word. He brings to memory verses I thought I'd long ago forgotten. It is amazing to me how He uses His Word at just the right time."

The internal movement of the soul that is

motivated by the Word is exemplified in a godly attitude, — "I will have respect unto Thy ways" (Ps. 119:15) and a godly walk, "I thought on my ways, and turned my feet unto Thy testimonies. I made haste, and delayed not to keep Thy commandments" (Ps. 119:59, 60).

God is not withdrawn far from us and wrapped in perpetual silence; He keeps watch over the smallest happenings on earth, and particularly those which affect His own children. God spoke not to Ephraim only but to all of us when He said, "I have written to him the great things of My law, but they were counted as a strange thing" (Hos. 8:12). God has given His Word, the pure water of life, and He takes particular notice of the believer's response to it. It must grieve Him exceedingly to observe those who count it "as a strange thing," by disregarding it because they seem to have no appetite for it.

It is good to read and study the Scriptures; it is better to memorize them and have them always instantly accessible. But we do not stop there; we must ever remember to be "doers of the Word, and not hearers only" (Jas. 1:22). The Word works effectually in a life when it is personally received, believed and appropriated as the very Word of God (1 Thess. 2:13). "Knowledge puffs up," and in the memorization of a large number of verses we must guard against pride by seeking diligently to appropriate those verses into a life which manifests the spirit of Christ. "He that is of God heareth God's words" (Jn. 8:47) and embraces them as his standard of holy living. He remains true to God amidst severe trials, and does not faint even while enduring the terrors of bitter persecution or the agony of much suffering.

Examples of Appropriating the Word

Many of us—young and older—have been strengthened by *Joni Eareckson Tada's* earnest testimony. She said in her book which she wrote by holding a pen in her mouth, "I memorized Scripture portions that had great meaning to me. Understanding these messages that spoke to me to better trust God with my will as well as my life. Even when distressing or despondent times came along, I could depend on the fact that 'He knew what He was doing,' as daddy frequently said. Through memorizing God's promises, I learned that the Lord would take me out of training in this school of suffering—but in his own time."

"He traineth thus
That we may teach the lessons we are taught
The younger learners may be further brought,

Led on by us.
Well may we wait, or toil, or suffer long
For His dear service to be made fit and strong."
— *Frances Ridley Havergal*

Many of us have been blessed by the testimony of *Eugene L. Clark* of *Back to the Bible Broadcast*. I had the joy of meeting him several years ago. Although crippled with arthritis and his body racked with pain, he never complains but continues with his service for the Lord. He wrote as follows: "Memorizing the Scripture under your plan during the past five years has been an immeasurable blessing. One reason that it cannot be measured is that by systematically memorizing the Word on a regular basis, we tend to absorb it into our lives and it becomes a part of us. I have found your plan challenging and workable. The attractive way in which the verses are presented and the incentives along the way have been extremely helpful and useful.

"About ten years ago I lost my eyesight and became bedfast with arthritis. Carrying on a useful ministry and raising a family of three children under these challenging conditions have led my wife, Ferne, and me to trust the Lord for many things and to re-evalulate our lives in the light of His Word. We are convinced that the effectiveness of a life or a ministry is directly related to its closeness to God's Word. The Lord instructed Joshua to meditate in His Word day and night and then he would have good success. This principle in Joshua chapter 1 was the experience of the Psalmist in Psalm 1 and reiterated by Jesus in His illustration of the vine and the branches in John chapter 15."

Each one of us must be fully convinced that as we treasure up God's Word we must not fail to appropriate it personally and allow God thus to perfect that which concerns us day by day. I recall reading about the minister who went to see an elderly lady. He asked for her Bible and began looking for some rich promises of God which he would read for her encouragement. Turning to one, he saw written in the margin "P," and he asked, "What does this mean?" "That means *precious*, sir." Turning the page, he saw "T and P," and he asked what those letters meant. "That means," she said with a gleam of joy on her face, "*tried and proved*; for I have tried and proved it in my own life."

So often, as Christians, we fail to use the precious promises that God has given us and this leads to failure almost without exception. Remember the incident in *Pilgrim's Progress* when *Christian* and *Hopeful* were in the dungeon of *Giant Despair*, and were advised by the Giant to commit suicide? The following conversation took place.

"At this they trembled greatly, and I think that Christian fell into a swoon; but coming a little to himself again, they renewed their discourse about the *Giant's* counsel; and whether they had best to take it or no. Now *Christian* again seemed to be for doing it, but *Hopeful* made his second reply as follows: 'My Brother,' said he, '*rememberest thou not how valiant thou hast been heretofore. Apollyon* could not crush thee, nor could all that thou didst hear, or see, or feel in the Valley of the Shadow of Death. . . . ' Well, on Saturday about midnight they began to pray and continued in Prayer till almost break of day. Now a little before it was day, good *Christian*, brake out in this passionate speech, 'What a fool,' said he, 'am I to lie in a stinking dungeon, when I may as well be at liberty! I have a key in my bosom, called *Promise*, that will, I am persuaded, open any Lock in *Doubting Castle*,' Then

150

said *Hopeful,* 'That's good news; good Brother pluck it out of thy bosom and try.'"

We are all engaged in a spiritual warfare — and our antagonists are not just flesh and blood, but they are subtle, strong and savage "principalities . . . powers . . . rulers of the darkness of this age . . . spiritual wickedness in high places" (Eph. 6:6-12). We need to discover as much as possible where our battleground lies and the nature of our spiritual struggle so that we may the more effectively appropriate the God-given armor in resisting the fiery darts and the pernicious onslaught of the devil. We would be strongly tempted to faint and give up at once if we did not realize the pertinent word from God which says, "Greater is He that is in you than he that is in the world" (1 Jn. 4:4). "Many times I have used the verses learned in your plan" writes *Don Sweaton* of Pensacola, "to resist the temptations of the devil."

The Word for Resisting Temptations

Let us *all* recognize that temptations of many varieties will come. They come *always* and they come to each one of us — young and older. Temptations originate within the heart of the sinner himself. It is useless for him to blame God. A person sins only when he is "enticed" by the bait, and "drawn away" by the hook of "his own lust." That lust includes the appetites of the body, the evil dispositions of the mind, such as pride, malice, envy, vanity, love of ease, etc.

Remember that the attacks of Satan are strong and savage, as he goes about seeking whom he may deceive and then devour. His strategies in tripping up the child of God and causing him to stumble and to sin are loaded with subtle allurements. He never gives up and his schemes are long-range, vicious and intent upon thwarting, if possible, God's purpose in our lives. The enemy approaches at one time in the heavy garb of carnality, "the lust of the flesh"; and in the next round he assumes the lighter robe of covetousness, "the lust of the eyes"; and then almost resembling the angel of light, he shows up in the delicate attire of vanity, "the pride of life"! But in all the many guises it is the same foe, the same devil. When we awake, he is there! When we move he follows! When we would do good, evil is present with us! The child of God is constantly pursued by the enemy of the ever-present temptations.

"Wretched man that I am," what shall I do? Scripture says, "Resist the devil, and he will flee from you" (Jas. 4:7). But remember, dear one, he is never frightened; he is not easily repulsed; therefore, be vigilant and resist him "steadfast in the faith . . ." and do not forget that "the God of all grace" is ever with you to "stablish, strengthen, settle you" (1 Pet. 5:8, 10).

In resisting temptation, keep that "sword of the spirit" polished bright! We can resist the devil and overcome temptations only as we "*take* the helmet of salvation, and the sword of the Spirit, which is the word of God" (Eph. 6:17).

Westcott points out that "the word of God" in Ephesians 6:17 means "a definite utterance of God." How wonderful it is to realize that we have for our own use the very same "sword" which our Lord used when He was under heavy attack from Satan (Matt. 4). That is why we must commit to memory these *definite divine utterances* so that they will be ready for use at the unexpected moment of need! Like a flash, we can thrust the sharp two-edged sword at the enemy of our souls!

One more thrilling observation! I believe it is in *Weymouth's* rendition that we find the note on the word "take" (Greek, *dechomai*) in Ephesians 6:17 to mean, "receive" as from the hand of God. *Bengel* confirms this meaning with "*receive* what is offered by the Lord."

Hallelujah! The light of this truth breaking through this poor human perception is like the brilliance of the sun bursting through the heavy clouds!

Yes, beloved, the temptations are sure to knock on our door, but you and I do not have to invite them in. We may, yea, we *can*, resist the devil by receiving from the Spirit of God that most appropriate divine "utterance," which we had so neatly filed in our memory; and suddenly that sword "wrought and edged by the Holy One Himself" (*Moule*) will be flashing and we shall know that we have "power . . . over all the power of the enemy" (Lu. 10:19).

Our God gives us the word. We *receive* it; we assimilate it; we meditate upon it; we *appropriate* it in that hour of temptation. And once that word is in our minds, let us hold it fast. "Take fast hold of instruction; let her not go: keep her; for she is thy life" (Prov. 4:13). This is how that truth in 1 Corinthians 10:13 works out in real life: "There is no temptation taken you but such as is common to man: but God is faithful, who will not suffer you to be tempted above that ye are able; but will with the temptation also make a way to escape, that ye may be able to bear it." God Himself has provided the way of escape from every temptation by the effectual use of His word (1 Thess. 2:13). Believest thou this?

Hundreds of experiences crowd upon the mind as to how believers in our generation, "obtain a good report through faith" in the Lord as a result of knowing and using His Word.

The Word for Cleansing

Let me ask the young men, the older men — yea, every believer: How can a believer cleanse his way and remain in fellowship with the Lord (Ps. 119:9; 1 Jn. 1:7, 8)? Is it by sheer determination never to commit sin? Indeed not! The cleansing comes from the Word. The Holy Spirit takes the quickening Word, enlightens the mind and probes the conscience as to God's remedy for sin's defilement. Then comes the contrite spirit, the humble confession! And the record says — "He," that is, God, "is faithful and just to forgive us our sins, and to cleanse us from all unrighteousness" (1 Jn. 1:9).

If the believer willfully persists to live in sin, God will deal with such a person as a father does with his son. "For whom the Lord loves He chastens, and scourges every son whom He receives" (Heb. 12:6). We all know how very true this is because of God's dealings with us and because we have observed His ways with others. At such a time, the person being thus disciplined who has the Word of God in mind and heart will respond to God more quickly and more wholeheartedly. He will realize that although "no chastening for the present seems to be joyous, but grievous: nevertheless afterward it yieldeth the peaceable fruit of righteousness unto them which are exercised thereby" (Heb. 12:11); he will not "despise" the "chastening of the Lord, nor faint" when he is "rebuked," of God (Heb. 12:5).

God's purpose in such dealings with His children is always with the view of restoration and also in order to prepare and mature them so that they may be understanding and better able, "in the spirit of meekness," to help restore others who have become "overtaken in a fault" (Gal. 6:1).

"Let each man, whether young or older," *Spurgeon* once admonished, "who desires to be holy, have a holy watchfulness in his heart, and keep his Holy Bible before his open eye." *David Livingstone* knelt down by his bedside at Ilala, Africa, as the rain dripped from the edges of his hut; he died on his knees with the open Bible before his face, humbly confessing his sin to God and praying yet again that the Spirit of God would continue to penetrate the darkness of Africa with the message of the Gospel.

The Word for Times of Severe Trial

In proclaiming the Word, the servant of the Lord shall often meet with severe trials and discouragements. He will find in those times of testing that his only resource is that precious Word of God which he has been recommending so zealously to others. How blessed it is at such times to be able to draw on God's own words of encouragement like those which were first spoken to Joshua, "Have not I commanded you? Be strong and of a good courage; be not afraid, neither be thou dismayed: for the Lord your God is with you whithersoever you go" (1:9). Varied needs will arise along the way but God knows that we have need of them, and makes thrilling provisions: "Thy shoes shall be iron and brass," He told the sons of Asher! Yes, but what about the aching feet, the feeble knees and the fainting body? What good are the "iron shoes"? Well, beloved, God is aware of that also, and He continues with His promise in the same verse, "and as thy days, so shall thy strength be." Praise the Lord! "Thou hast delivered my soul from death," the Psalmist said, "my eyes from tears, and my feet from falling. I will walk before the Lord in the land of the living" (Ps. 116:8, 9).

The servant is renewed and other wonderful promises come to mind: "I will go in the strength of the Lord" (Ps. 71:16); "I can do all things through Christ who strengthens me" (Phil. 4:13). And if the response to his earnest efforts at times appears to be unrewarding, he takes fresh courage as he remembers God's promise in Isaiah 55:11, "My word . . . shall not return unto me void."

The Word for Seasons of Deep Depression

There is many a person who has experienced tragic disappointment in his brethren, and is enduring unspeakable depression which envelops him in darkness like a thick cloud, and continues persistently to obscure all hope. He may be too "overwhelmed" within his spirit (Ps. 143:4) to read the Word, but as he struggles in the darkness he seems to see emblazoned on the wall in front of him, "*You will keep him in perfect peace, whose mind is stayed on You, because he trusts in You!*" (Isa. 26:3). "Perfect peace" — why, that's exactly what he does *not* have! What's the trouble? Why does he not have that "perfect peace"? Oh, the "mind." Where is it? It must be "stayed on Him." What is that mind

occupied with? What is that mind contem-
plating?

Dear friend, let me tell you, *refuse to dwell*
on those disappointments! Let that *mind* be
steadily "stayed" on the Lord. And then you
will hear the parting words of our blessed Lord
just as if He was right there in the room with
you, "Peace I leave with you, My peace I give
unto you" (Jn. 14:27).

Oh, yes, he needs that peace, but everything has turned against him. The Lord continues, though, "not as the world gives, give I
unto you." The world affords a measure of
quietness when all speak well of you and all
the circumstances are favorable, but all that
sense of well-being is gone when the storm hits.
But the peace of our Lord does not depend upon
circumstances; it comes strictly as a result of
our relationship to Him! Say those words again,
beloved! *"Peace I leave with you, My peace I give
unto you: not as the world gives, give I unto you."*
Say them out loud! Say them yet again until
you can quietly relax, and then joyfully complete the rest of the verse, *"Let not your heart be
troubled, neither let it be afraid"* (Jn. 14:27).

"Weeping may endure for a night" — that
night may be long — it may last weeks and

months — "but joy comes in the morning" (Ps. 30:5). Yes, and some golden daybreak Jesus will come, and all will be only glory! Only glory bye and bye!

How wonderful, how blessed it is to have that Word in your mind and heart! Because, *perhaps when you need that Word the most*, you do not have the desire nor even the strength to reach for the Bible. But when that Word is written upon your heart, you can lay hold of it like a flash. You may be pinned under that car or tractor and not have the opportunity to turn the pages of the Book, but the Holy Spirit will bring just the right word to your remembrance if you take time to memorize it.

The Word for Wisdom

Here is another saint who must make an important decision. He needs wisdom! So much depends upon this particular step. He must know what the mind of the Lord is. He cannot afford to make a mistake. Then, he remembers the word of James, "If any of you lack wisdom, let him ask of God." What will God do? He "gives to *all* men liberally" (that "all" includes all who ask in faith) "and upbraids not, and it shall be given him" (Jas. 1:5). God gives wisdom! What kind of wisdom is it? How does

God react to hard-headed people, to knotty circumstances? Well, remember James 3:17, "But the wisdom that is from above is first pure, then peaceable, gentle, and easy to be entreated, full of mercy and good fruits, without partiality and without hypocrisy." *Thank you, Lord*! This is to the believer the most satisfying and God-like description of that "wisdom from above." It is so definitive, so superlatively complete! Oh, that God might so tune our minds with Himself that in all our dealings with others we may think, react and speak, in a quiet and "gentle" manner, words that are "pure"; that our attitudes would not be adamant, but that we might be easily entreated; that we might not push justice until it screams, but be overflowing with "mercy and good fruits," and in every respect be free from "partiality and hypocrisy."

The Word for Comfort

There are always those about us whose eyes are swimming in tears, amidst deep sorrow and grief "concerning them which are asleep." The "God of all comfort" would remind all such that we "sorrow not for others which have no hope." The trumpet shall sound; the Lord shall return with the saints who have gone to heaven, and we "shall be caught up together with them in the clouds, to meet the Lord in the air: and so shall we ever be with the Lord. Wherefore comfort one another with these words" (1 Thess. 4:13-18). A dear sister, *Hermine Bauer-Emmert*—just asked me on the phone, "Is the time of His coming very near?"

The Word for Joy Amidst Poverty and Pain

Or it may be poverty, privations, pain and sickness that are holding you in their threatening grasp: Think now! Think of that verse you memorized in Psalm 37—"*Rest in the Lord*"—just let go and let God—"Rest in the Lord and wait patiently for him." Remember, *remember* the words of our Lord when He said, "Come unto Me all you that labor and are heavy laden and I will give you rest" (Matt. 11:28). And as you keep *looking unto Jesus*, you may reach that glorious *yet* of Habakkuk: "Although the fig tree shall not blossom, neither shall fruit be in the vines; the labor of the olive shall fail, and the fields shall yield no meat; the flock shall be cut off from the fold, and there shall be no herd in the stalls: YET I will rejoice in the Lord, I will joy in the God of my salvation (3:17, 18).

YET . . . Despite all the adversities and in the midst of them, "yet I will rejoice in the Lord."

162

Say it with the prophet, "*Yet, I will rejoice in the Lord, I will joy in the God of my salvation*" (3:18).

My friends, the memorized Word of God will do its mighty work in every field of battle when by the Spirit of God it is accepted and applied!

All of us, without exception, do battle in the thought-life. And His purpose is that there would be on the part of every believer the "bringing into captivity every thought to the obedience of Christ" (2 Cor. 10:5). God looks less upon the outside of life; He goes straight home to the hearts of men, for "as he thinks in his heart, so is he" (Prov. 23:7). In one of his God-breathed epistles, the Apostle Paul lays out a formula for the thought-life: "Finally, brethren, whatsoever things are true, whatsoever things are honest, whatsoever things are just, whatsoever things are pure, whatsoever things are lovely, whatsoever things are of good report; if there be any virtue, and if there be any praise, think on these things" (Phil. 4:8). The Apostle says, "think on these things"! He lays emphasis not on our conduct, but on our deeper thought. It is not the dirt on our hands, nor the unclean food that defiles a man, but it is the evil thoughts!

God sets about us the whole circle of perfection, and says, *think* on these things. If you awake in the night, *think* upon them! In the car, bus, or plane, *think* upon them. In your work, in your school, in your home, let the things of God that are pure and honorable, and just, and lovely rule all your thoughts and keep your heart enthralled with the things that God has for us.

Wouldn't that be a wonderful life? But how can we succeed in doing it? We have all tried. We have all failed. We have all had to confess that we have fallen short. We certainly will not succeed by setting ourselves to wage a negative battle against things that are untrue, and impure, and unlovely, and of evil report. The more we struggle with these evils, the more deeply will they sink their tentacles into our minds and hearts.

There is only one way of victory in this arena! We can only think upon these things, I believe, by becoming occupied and enamored completely with the One who is truth, Who is absolutely honest, Who is perfectly just, Who alone is pure, Who is "altogether lovely," and utterly without blemish — the wonderful Lord of glory!

Why should we not desire and seek such complete devotion to Him and so love Him when we know how much He first loved us? Why should we not have still just such passion after Christ as did the saints of old?

My friends, the path of such love and such intimate fellowship with our blessed Lord is one that will be laid out before us with stepping stones and hedges that are clearly marked by the memorized Scriptures which in the volume of the whole Book, speak of Him. Our meditation of Him shall be sweet, and we shall increasingly find ourselves thinking upon things that are true, honest, just, pure, lovely and of good report!

Frequently, I am asked if I memorized the Scriptures which I arrange and recommend to others. The answer is positively, *yes!* Furthermore, I believe that every Christian worker should read, study and MEMORIZE the Word. "The husbandman that labors must be first partaker of the fruits" (2 Tim. 2:6). The blessed Word of God has always been the greatest spiritual resource in my ministry. The times I have faltered can be readily traced to the fact that I have failed to claim the promises of God for the needed strength.

Those Who Memorize Reap the Blessings

Through the years, thousands of people have written to express the blessings and benefits that they have experienced through Bible memorization. Let me just cite a few:

1) *Mrs. Dan Graves*, Memphis, wrote: "May I relate one of the wonderful things that happened? Our seven-year-old son memorized Elementary Book 1. As he was working in his bedroom on lesson 9, 'The Lord Died For Me' (Rom. 5:8), he came into the living room with tears in his eyes and told me how he wanted to become a Christian right then. He did so, and immediately started asking when a relative (whom I have been praying for) was going to become a Christian."

2) "It was not until I began to 'eat' God's Word by memorizing it," writes *Mrs. Frances Nebel* of St. Louis, "that I really started maturing spiritually." Scripture memorizing does indeed help a Christian *to come alive*!

3) "I am amazed at the transforming power in these verses as they are committed to memory. They become a part of my being, of my *well-being*. The Holy Spirit gives life by the Word, 2 Cor. 3:6" (*Mrs. S. A. Franks*, Ridgecrest, CA).

4) "I try to pray very often that the Holy Spirit will teach the Bible memorizers throughout America the meaning of the verses they learn, so that their understanding may be enlightened," said *Miss Vivian Braithwaite*, of Seattle, who has herself memorized in this systematic way since she was a small child.

5) "*The finger of God* seemed to point at me from each verse I memorized to show me my need or to bless me" (*Mrs. Richard Bell*, Kansas City).

6) *The Team Mission* recently carried an interesting story about *Mr. George Darquea* who came from Colombia, South America and was introduced to our system of memorizing the Word by *Jay Lake* at a clothing store in Wheaton, Illinois. George was not a Christian at the time. His wife, *Dura*, and their six children were still in Bogota, Colombia. George faced many tough problems, but each week he went to Jay's home to recite the verses and talk about them. Soon George became a Christian, his wife and family joined him in Wheaton, and one time after reciting the Scriptures prescribed for that week, George said to Jay: "You know, these Bible verses have *comforted* me so much. I never could have

gone on with all the problems I've had if it hadn't been for this experience learning the Word of God."

Scores of friends, both young and old, write to tell how the memorized Word stimulates and strengthens their prayer life. I recall reading about the young lady who was the average kind of church member. She said to her pastor one day, "After all is it not just as well to talk *about* God as to talk *to* God?" The pastor replied, "How is it about your mother? Is it just as well to talk *about* your mother as it is to talk *to* her?" "Oh no," she said, "that is different. Mother talks back you know." This is precisely the vital part of talking with God. He desires to talk back to us. Praying is not just spreading our wants before Him, and then running off before He has time to say anything to us, although, unfortunately, this is what so often happens. After we have prayed, we should say, as did the handmaid of old, "Let my Lord the King now speak" (2 Sam. 14:18). So often, we kneel down and go through our prayer requests with considerable earnestness and meaning, but then we quickly rush away from the King's presence as soon as we have had our say and hardly expected Him to send His answers, Surely, He had something to say

168

to us but we never waited a minute to see and to hear what His gracious response would be.

"Master, speak! Thy servant hears,
Waiting for Thy gracious word.
Longing for Thy voice that cheers;
Master! let it now be heard."
— *Frances Ridley Havergal*

How marvelously the two-way conversation of prayer is facilitated when we have God's words already imprinted upon our minds. Right now we are in great need! Probably everyone who reads this is weighed down with burdens which are being spread before the Lord in prayer.

A very familiar verse is looming larger and larger before me these days. It is Jeremiah 33:3:

"Call unto Me, and I will answer you, and show you great and mighty things which you know not."

We have been calling and we know that God will answer and give us a gracious and unexpected reply (Jer. 29:11).

Our gracious God invites us to pray, and then He immediately tells us what He is going to do about it! If He tells us that He will wait, it is in order "that He may be gracious unto us."

He reminds us to maintain our implicit trust in Him when He says, "Blessed are all they that wait for Him" (Isa. 30:18). He does not desire His children to become impatient with Him. We do not know exactly *how* or *when* He will answer, but He Himself assures us that the answer will come and it will be very substantial and satisfying, to say the least. And is it not just simply "super" as the younger set would say, to have those sure words from God neatly placed in our memory. I think that it is most gratifying to God to realize that we do have them indelibly written in our minds and to hear us articulating them to Him in a spirit of triumphing hope and faith! Hallelujah! God is good! His Word is true, and we are spiritual millionaires!

What then shall these millionaires do next?

I must relate briefly *Captain James E. Ray's* (Conroe, Texas), thrilling account of how the remembered Scriptures kept the men in the Hanoi prison from going mad or becoming animals, "One night I lay with my ear pressed against the wall to hear 'thump . . . thumpety thump' as somewhere on the wall a fellow P.O.W. tapped out in Morse code: 'I will lift up mine eyes unto the hills, from whence comes my help' (Ps. 121:1). Another time a verse I heard thumped out was: 'Man shall not live by bread alone, but by every word that proceeds out of the mouth of the Lord.' "

"The men began to pool the verses they could recall and thus have a 'consensus Bible' among them. After many months of pleading, the 'Hanoi Hilton' commander let us have a copy of the King James Bible for 'one hour' each week." Captain Ray made this keen observation, "Bible verses on paper aren't one iota as useful as Scriptures burned into your mind where you can draw on them for guidance and comfort."

Remembering and Believing

Appropriation of the Word depends so much on two things: *remembering and believing!*

The children of Israel were reminded of God's miraculous works in delivering them from the bondage in Egypt (Ps. 106:1-11). Then, somehow their memory faded. Cares and disappointments moved in, and they "forgot His works: they waited not for His counsel" (106:13). The ways of the flesh followed: They lusted, they envied, they promoted idolatry, "they forgot God their savior. . . ." (106:21). ". . . they despised the pleasant land." Then comes the record of their condition which was the reason for their serious defections: "They believed not His word," and instead of praising Him they "murmered in their tents, and hearkened not unto the voice of the Lord" (106:24, 25).

Spiritual leanness always follows when we neglect God's Word and forget His manifold works of grace. May the Lord quicken our minds and help us each day to do our part by "gathering up the forces of memory," and causing His word to dwell richly in our hearts in all wisdom (Col. 3:16), so that we may *remember* all the way which the Lord our God has led us, protected us and provided for us in our pilgrim journey. ". . . there has not failed one word of all his good promise . . ." (1 Kings 8:56).

"Hear, O my son, and receive my sayings;
and the years of thy life shall be many.

I have taught you in the way of wisdom;
I have led you in right paths.

When you go, your steps shall not be straitened;
and when you run, you shall not stumble"
(Prov. 4:10-12).

Chapter Eleven

PROPAGATION ... of the WORD

Propagation — spreading the Word of God to others is the added blessing that comes as a result of assimilating the Scriptures. You soon find out like Jeremiah (Ch. 20) that you just cannot keep the mighty Word of God stashed away quietly in your own life. It will be like a fountain of living water springing up continually (Jn. 4:14) and forming "rivers of living water," which by the power of the Holy Spirit, will "flow" on and on and bless many lives in its course.

There will be opportunities of quoting the

Word in personal conversations, and just as often there will be the opportunity to explain the meaning of the Word. Many young people and adults use the learning process as a very effective means of giving the message out to others. Simply hand your Memory Book to a friend — in school, on the bus, at work — and ask him to check and see if you are reviewing them correctly. He will be glad to oblige even though he may be just a bit suspicious that you are doing it for his benefit. Many times the person will ask questions and you will be thrilled to see how the answers will be forthcoming from the Word.

Not long ago I received a report from *Mrs. Fred Erickson* of Portland, Oregon, which relates precisely this very kind of result. "First, *we have good news!* If one of our adult reciters hasn't written you, we want to report a lady being saved through your memorization system! *Mrs. Schreiner* has been witnessing to an Arab neighbor lady for two years and praying for her. *Dorothy Schreiner* decided to ask this lady to hear her verses twice a week and she agreed to (Basic Adult 1). The Scriptures made the listener aware that her own good works she'd been counting on weren't good enough for God. She read the notes and asked questions which Dorothy answered with verses from the first two—three lessons. Two days before Christmas the neighbor accepted the Lord and we are all thrilled."

Witnessing as You Memorize and Recite

Reciting the verses to your friends and others is a very good way to review the verses, and explaining their meaning gives you a deeper understanding and appreciation of them. This type of fellowship certainly becomes an occasion for you to share your love for the things of God and how your own life in Christ has been growing richer and more fruitful as you have the Scriptures engraved on your heart. In it all, you must always remember not to draw attention to yourself or the number of verses you have memorized, but exalt the Lord Jesus Christ. Use the Scriptures to make Him real and precious.

Folks will be drawn to Him by the magnetism and radiance of His presence and power manifest in your life. They will discover that it is not just another program that you are promoting, but that it is a living Person, Christ Jesus the Lord, Whom you are seeking to make known. Ask God to help you find new and creative ways of sharing the Word with others, according to your own personality and lifestyle.

Then by all means take the offensive and

encourage your friend to get started in a systematic way of memorizing the Word. Of course you will listen understandingly to the standard excuses, but you will the more enthusiastically continue to challenge your friend, neighbor or acquaintance to get started in a spiritual diet program that will become one of the most important things in his whole life.

Seek opportunities to promote Scripture memorizing in Sunday School, in Bible study groups, in youth fellowships, Christian schools and wherever doors are opened. God wonderfully blesses and rewards every such effort. Hundreds of times I have heard folks say in different places, "You know, it was *Brother Stone*, or *Mrs. Love*, or *Mrs. Walker*, or my college chum, *Cliff*, who first got me started memorizing the Word in this systematic way, and because of it, hearts will continue to be spiritually enriched and thanksgiving to God will abound yet more and more.

It is truly amazing how the Spirit of God opens the doors of opportunity when we are filled with the Word and overflowing with His love. I just came across a word from *Mrs. Del Pain*, down in Costa Rica. She said, "My husband has been trying to sell the idea of your systematic Scripture memorization to other missionaries down here, and I want to take this opportunity once again to express my appreciation for all you have done. These verses have been a real enlightenment to my own heart and in using them doors have been opened in witnessing to others."

Another interesting story comes from *Mrs. Jerry Romprey* in Sweden, "Our family sat together having our usual 'family devotions' last Monday night, only we had a guest—an unsaved nurse I met, witnessed to and invited to eat with us. The Lord led us to talk with her regarding salvation. I was trying to think of a certain verse when *Glenn* (who is an Elementary 4 contestant) suddenly quoted it perfectly from an earlier assignment. He was so thrilled to be of help, and we all rejoiced later when she invited Christ to save her!"

I remember two or three years ago reading a letter from a missionary in Nairobi, Kenya, whose little boy was memorizing Scripture verses from the ABC Book. Some relatives who had three boys came to visit them, she said, and the boys were rowdy and paid no attention to the admonitions of the parents. Things were getting progressively worse, when suddenly her son stood up before the three ill-disciplined noise-makers and pointed his finger at them he said in a firm voice, "C. . . . Children obey your parents in the Lord, for this is right." She said a strange hush came over the unruly chaps and all the adults took real notice of what had happened. The missionary said she was very grateful to the Lord, "not only because her child was hiding God's Word in his heart, but that even at his early age he understood its meaning and was able to use it so effectually and quite unexpectedly."

Then an interesting report from *Mrs. R. D. Robinson* in Abilene, Texas, who told us how their five year old boy used one of the verses he had memorized on his "growling" kitten: "This new ABC plan is just marvelous," she said: "Our youngest memorized it last year. He loved it and can still say his verses from last year. His favorite book is his Memory Book. He even used some of the Scripture on his kitten, which growled a lot one morning. Philip said in a very determined voice, 'K. . . . Keep your tongue from evil.' We were all amazed that he could not only remember a verse, but be able to apply it to a home situation."

Timothy's Example

There is another boy that I want to mention in this connection. His name is Timothy and the great Apostle Paul *claimed* him as "my dearly beloved son" (2 Tim. 1:2).

Important as Paul's influence was on Timothy, the tenor of the Scriptures in 2 Timothy 3 would seem to suggest that the Apostle is particularly reminding his young fellow-laborer in the Gospel regarding the untarnished spiritual heritage that he had in his godly mother and grandmother. They were good women, noted for their "unfeigned faith" (2 Tim. 1:5). They first held the young child on their knees and lovingly guided his little finger in tracing out the "Sacred letters." They trained his seeking young mind in the Holy Scriptures." They would not misrepresent, nor exaggerate, nor neglect anything that pertained to his spiritual training.

Timothy is called upon to reflect upon his Bible-learning with confidence and with a becoming sense of gratitude to God. *"But continue thou in the things which thou hast learned and has been assured of, knowing of whom thou hast learned them"* (2 Tim. 3:14). He had been taught the Scriptures from *his very infancy* (the original word here is 'brephos'). As soon as he was capable of learning anything at all, his mother Eunice and his grandmother Lois drilled him in the Old Testament Scriptures; as yet the New Testament Scriptures were unavailable. Timothy had a devout mother and it was customary in such homes to tutor their young children in the Scriptures. The Jewish writings abound with such examples. A certain *Rabbi Judah* writes, "The boy of five years of age ought to apply to the study of the sacred Scriptures.".

The "sacred writings" or "sacred letters," which is the unusual choice of words here for the "Holy Scriptures," convey the thought that little "Tim" learned his ABC's from the Bible. He probably learned to recognize letters through use of the Bible. This is much more wonderful than the practice of our day which supplies secular matters for the primers, and puts off the "sacred letters" until later years, which too often never come. From his very infancy, Timothy was saturated with God's Word.

And so it is quite natural that the aged Apostle in the closing chapter of his last epistle would turn to Timothy, his closest associate in the work of the Lord, and plead with him most earnestly for the sake of the Gospel: *"I charge thee*, therefore, before God. . ." (2 Tim. 4:1). Paul delivered this solemn charge to Timothy, "before" God — literally, in full view of God. With the vision of the Judge of the universe before his eyes, the Apostle lays his earnest testimony upon the young man's heart. He is intensely solicitous that the work of the Gospel should go on with undiminished force after his death.

The charge is then stated; it is an imperative command to every child of God: "Preach the word; be instant in season, out of season; reprove, rebuke exhort with all longsuffering and doctrine" (2 Tim. 4:2). Three mighty words, *"Preach the word!"* Go quickly as God's herald and deliver to the people God's message of redeeming grace. This is the pattern for every preacher and every witness today, whether he be in the pulpit, in the pew or in the factory. He is God's herald. He is under divine authority to proclaim God's message. Like the Emperor's herald he dare not withhold, nor revise, nor delay, nor neglect the message. He must announce it in its completeness irrespective of conditions or his own likes or dislikes. The Apostle bears his own testimony in this respect when he said to the Ephesian elders, "For I have not shunned to declare unto you all the counsel of God" (Acts 20:27).

Go as God's herald, and deliver to the people God's message. Cry like a common crier in the hearing of the multitude. This is what God said to Isaiah, "Cry aloud, spare not, lift up thy voice like a trumpet" (58:1).

The "Word" is the body of truth—Gospel truth—that Paul has said so much about in these two epistles to Timothy. It refers to the whole body of revealed truth (Gal. 6:6; 1 Thess. 1:6). God's witness is to proclaim the exact message his Sovereign gave him to proclaim. It is the living, abiding, unerring Word, which we call the Bible. It is God's infallible revelation. It is his declaration of unchanging truth. It is forever set up in heaven (Ps. 119:89). It is the divine Constitution and Bylaws for all time. This then is the message the servant of God must proclaim—not his own ideas, not book reviews, not politics, not psychology, not the current topics of the day, not the grandiose schemes of churchmen, nor even the cherished programs of his own organization. God's herald is commissioned to declare *God's* message— nothing more and nothing less.

And who is better fitted, better qualified, better commissioned and more completely and more fully obligated to do so than the ones like

Timothy, who have been treasuring up God's Word in their hearts!

Speak it out! There will always be some who will hear and who will heed!

"He that hath My word, let him speak My word faithfully" (Jer. 23:28).

The enemy increasingly spouts out and spreads the hellish, destructive ideas and philosophies — promoted by Satan — and there is always so much worthless stuff polluting the air waves! — Speak out the truth! "What is the chaff to the wheat?" saith the Lord. "Is not my word like as a fire?" saith the Lord, "and like a hammer that breaks the rock in pieces?" "I am against the prophets," says the Lord, "that steal my words. . . . that prophesy false dreams. . . . and cause my people to err by their lies" (Jer. 23:28-32).

There is supernatural power in this wonderful Word of God and although unbelievers, skeptics and atheists have tried to destroy it through the centuries, still it survives and is blessed of God in the life of everyone that receives it.

When the Scottish missionary, *Alexander Duff,* (1806-1878), sailed for India in 1829, the ship in which he traveled was wrecked. The young missionary had with him 800 volumes of choice books; all were lost. The disconsolate group of survivors stood safely on the shore, but all their possessions were gone. They looked to the sea from the shoreline, hoping that some of their belongings might be salvaged. Only one small object was seen bobbing up and down in the waters. It was Duff's Bible. The incident was symbolic of the survival of God's Word—a survival so miraculous that it can be explained only by Divine Providence. God's Word is eternal!

Chapter Twelve

DELECTATION . . . in the WORD

Delectation! The word means *holy delight;* and although at first it seems undesirable, the word is percisely correct even though it still seems inadequate to describe that overpowering sense of heavenly joy and inexpressible delight that floods our souls after a season of undistracted meditation upon the memorized Word of God. This reaction most of us have experienced and in every instance found ourselves quite incapable of expressing the depths of spiritual blessing that we enjoyed. We see these kinds of exclamations over and over again throughout the Book of Psalms and in other portions of Scripture. Join the Psalmist as he exults in the Word:

"The law of Thy mouth is better unto me than thousands of gold and silver" (Ps. 119:72).

"Unless Thy law had been my delights, I should then have perished in my affliction. I will never forget Your precepts: for with them You have quickened me" (Ps. 119:92, 93).

"Your testimonies have I taken as a heritage for ever: for they are the rejoicing of my heart" (Ps. 119:111).

"Your word is very pure: therefore your servant loves it" (Ps. 119:140).

"Consider how I love Your precepts: quicken me, O Lord, according to Your lovingkindness. Your word is true from the beginning: and every one of Your righteous judgments endure forever" (Ps. 119:159, 160).

"Seven times a day do I praise You because of Your righteous judgments.

*Great peace have they which love Your
law: nothing shall offend them"*
(Ps. 119: 164, 165).

When our attention is fully focused upon
the Word of the Lord, we exclaim it, we repeat
it, and we find unspeakable satisfaction as our
whole being is drawn into the most intimate
communion with our great God and Savior,
Jesus Christ! This is probably what the Psalmist
was trying to convey when he said, "I will delight myself in Your statutes." The expression
is very emphatic and means literally, "I will skip
about and jump for joy."

Meditation on the Word does not always
bring such radiant joy; it is not automatic; it is
not likely that it can be cultivated. It comes un-
bidden! It is really the overflowing of the blessed
Holy Spirit; and when it does come, we feel like
we are in another world, lifted up into the sub-
urbs of heaven! It is not likely that this intense
degree of joy will remain indefinitely at the high
level—we could hardly contain it—but there is
one effect that will always stay with us and the
Psalmist makes note of it thus, "I will not forget
Your Word" (Ps. 119:16). *Delectation* strengthens the memory, and the memory again renews
meditation. I see this cycle of blessing in a

testimony from *Mrs. Helen Sather*, of San Diego, "As I memorize I grow in grace and as I grow I have greater desire to memorize God's Word. I am indeed abundantly blest! It would thrill you to see and hear twelve year old David using Scripture he has learned in your system to exalt his Lord and to witness to others. He just simply bubbles over."

The significant aspect of this rapturous delight is its spontaneity. It does not seem to depend upon outward circumstances, but just springs up as we comtemplate the Word of God. We can hardly fail to observe the fact that the upspringing of this celestial joy is the blessed Holy Spirit moving our hearts and minds by the use of the written Word, which we have in our minds and heart.

Memorizing the Word and Being Filled With the Spirit

Believers are commanded to be *filled with the Spirit*: "And be not drunk with wine wherein is excess; but be filled with the Spirit" (Eph. 5:18). The unsaved often turn to strong drink for physical stimulation and for relief from the burdens of the day and then find themselves only further depleted and dissipated. By way of direct contrast, God has something infinitely superior for the one who is born of God: *"Be filled with the Spirit."* The influence of strong drink makes a person irrational and erratic, and leaves him in a state of dejection. Being filled with the Spirit makes the child of God rational, calm and joyful.

The Scripture which commands the filling by the Spirit is followed by five participles (two of them go together) which describe four very distinctive qualities of the life which characterizes the believer who is filled with the Spirit (Eph. 5:18-22). Consider them carefully:

1) *"Speaking to yourselves in psalms and hymns and spiritual songs."* The saints who are filled with the Spirit are exhorted to speak to one another intelligibly, using psalms and hymns and spiritual songs, and in a manner so as to edify one another (1 Cor. 14:26). It cannot be emphasized too strongly that the Psalms we can best use in this manner are not just those which are in the Book but those which have been stored up in the heart through diligent memorization and which are instantly and constantly accessible for such use, day and night. This is the point that *Carole Lewis*, of Memphis wanted to make when she wrote: "The wonderful thing about hiding the Scriptures in your heart is that they

are always there when you need them." And we might add the fact that they are there for the Holy Spirit to use in our lives in those particular situations when we may not be aware of our acute need.

2) *"Singing and making melody in your heart to the Lord."* This is the experience of that celestial joy—"joy unspeakable and full of glory" (1 Pet. 1:8). Is it not really the joy of the Lord that floods our souls as we think upon His Word? Remember John 15:11? "These things I have spoken unto you, that my joy might remain in you, and that your joy might be full."

3) *"Giving thanks always for all things."* Another quality of the Spirit-filled life is the ability to give thanks to God, not only for the blessings He bestows, but also for *all* the experiences of life—the triumphs and defeats, the joys and the sorrows—which our heavenly Father providentially brings into our lives. It is His will that we give thanks "in everything" (1 Thess. 5:18).

4) *"Submitting yourselves one to another."* There is always to be a happy harmony in the home and in the fellowship of God's people working together. No rivalry, no pride, no self-exaltation! Each is to submit himself voluntarily for the Lord's

sake. Obviously such harmony and fellowship will not exist unless each believer is continually submitting himself to the will of God.

Now the big question is how can a Christian be filled with the Spirit! I believe that we will find a clear answer to this basic question by comparing two Scriptures; in writing to the *Colossians* in a context similar to that of Ephesians 5:18-21, the Apostle Paul said: "Let the word of Christ dwell in you richly in all wisdom; teaching and admonishing one another in psalms and hymns and spiritual songs, singing with grace in your hearts to the Lord" (3:16). This not only helps to clear up some of the details in the Ephesian passage, but it supplies an unmistakable lead regarding a necessary condition for the filling with the Holy Spirit. You will observe that to the Ephesians Paul said, "*Be filled with the Spirit.*" Then, quite obviulsy in a similar context the Apostle said to the Colossians, "Let the word of Christ dwell in you richly." The inescapable conclusion is that being filled with the Spirit and being filled with the Word of God are *absolutely inseparable.* A person cannot really be filled with the Spirit who does not have the Word of God filling his mind and heart continually. Thus, the filling with the Spirit becomes a solid, abiding reality and not just an occasional experience stimulated by feelings, and primed by emotional group therapy.

This is all so exceedingly important. It is quite useless for a believer to say that he is filled with the Spirit unless he is full of the Word of God. Our Lord said, "The words that I speak unto you, they are spirit, and they are life" (Jn. 6:63).

Let us pause here and with all the sense of delight and appreciation that we can muster, let us exclaim with the psalmist:

"O how love I Thy law!
it is my meditation all the day" (Ps. 119:97).

How very excellent and wonderful is the word of God! "I will worship toward Your holy temple, and praise Your name for Your lovingkindness and for Your truth: for You have magnified Your word above all Your name" (Ps. 138:2). And in Isaiah 55:8-11, God sets forth the infinite superiority of the Word of God as compared with the concepts and ways of men:

For My thoughts are not your thoughts,
neither are your ways My ways, says
the Lord.

For as the heavens are higher than the
earth, So are My ways higher than your

192

ways,and My thoughts than your thoughts.

For as the rain comes down, and the snow from heaven, and do not return there, but waters the earth, and makes it bring forth and bud, that it may give seed to the sower, and bread to the eater: so shall My word be that goes forth out of My mouth: it shall not return unto Me void, but it shall accomplish that which I please, and it shall prosper in the thing whereto I sent it.

I remember several years ago, returning from Brazil aboard a small passenger-cargo ship, which had about one hundred and twenty-five passengers. The trip normally took about fourteen days, and because of a longshoremen's strike along the East Coast, the ship was docked at the Island of Curacao in the Netherland Antilles for about an additional five days. On a long voyage, you get to know the people rather intimately.

I remember in particular the couple from Boston, Massachuetts, who visited with me quite frequently. When they discovered that I had majored in English literature at Baylor University, they began to ask me various questions. I recall that Mrs. "Boston," who seemed to take herself quite seriously, was walking around with a book titled, I believe, *Which Side Is Up*—a very profound subject.

She would engage me in conversation, along these lines: "Have you read such and such a book?" and I would say, "No, I haven't; and then she would ask the same question and refer me to another book and each time, somewhat reluctantly, I would answer, "No, I have not even heard of it." Apparently she belonged to some book of the month club and was reading them quite regularly. I don't read them—nor do I even look over the condensations of those books—and every time that I would answer negatively or say, "I have never heard of it," she would say, "Oh, my!" She deplored my literary limitations. She began to speak of certain authors inasmuch as her son was a publisher in New York City and, of course, I wasn't acquainted with the authors of his books either. She seemed quite elated with her triumph over me and continued reading *Which Side Is Up*.

So, I thought about it, prayed, and then the next time I saw them, I took the offensive, and said to her, "Mrs. 'Boston,' do you think that *John Milton* ever finished writing *Paradise Regained*?" And she said, "Well, I don't know whether he did or not; what do you think about it?" That was a trap that I was preparing for her and she asked the right questions! I said, "Well, I don't think he ever finished it. As a matter of fact, when I read it, I wrote in the margin, 'This is not completed!' I believe that in his blindness and sickness, he became discouraged and never finished writing what he intended to include in *Paradise Regained*." Then, she said, "Well, what makes you think so?" At that point, she stepped right into the "trap." I was hoping that she would ask precisely that question. And I said, "Well, because the questions and problems that are anticipated in *Paradise Lost* are not fully answered in *Paradise Regained*." She looked puzzled, and I proceeded, "You, have read *Paradise Lost*, haven't you?" And she said, "No, I haven't!" I said, "*My!* outside the Bible that is about the greatest thing that has ever been written."

Then I pursued it a bit further and said to her, "What do you think of *Robert Browning*? Do you believe that he is really obscure in his writing or is it that people try to read him like they would read a fiction book?" Well, she didn't know. I said, "What do you think of *Wordsworth* as a poet? Was he a pantheist or did he just appreciate God through nature?" I continued, "You have read his *Prelude* and *Excursion*, have you not?" She said, "No, I have not." And I said, "*My!*" And then I went on and said, "Have you read Spencer's *Fairy Queen?*" "No," she said, rather peevishly, "I haven't." "Well," I said, "it's a bit difficult to comprehend."

And then I started out with these words:

*"What that Aprille with hise shoures soote
The droghte of March hath perced to the roote,
And bathed every veyne in swich licour
Of which vertu engendred is the flour."*

She was rather confused and thought that probably I was speaking in some strange tongue. I happened to remember those four lines from Chaucer's *Canterbury Tales* and made some considerable mileage from it that day!

She was ready to go, but I said, "Now, Mrs. 'Boston,' I have said all these things in order that I might be able to say something much more important, and it is this. You have been talking to me these days about one kind of writings of men, and today I have been talking with you concerning another kind of literature, which I think is superior inasmuch as it has already established itself as something which, no doubt, will live much longer. "But," I said, "there is yet a third kind of writing which is much, much superior to everything else that we have mentioned in our conversations."

She asked, "What is that?" I responded, "I am referring to the writings which have been inspired by God" and which are infinitely superior to the words of men: 'For as the heavens are higher than the earth, so are My ways higher than your ways, and My thoughts than your thoughts .' (Isa. 55:8, 9). Then I followed up quickly by asking, "Have you ever heard of the upper room discourse?" "No," she said, "I haven't." I said, "Would you like to hear a little of it?" "Well, go ahead," she said. So I proceeded with those incomparable words of our Lord:

"Let not your heart be troubled:
You believe in God, believe also in Me.

In My Father's house are many mansions:
if it were not so, I would have told you.
I go to prepare a place for you.

And if I go and prepare a place for you,
I will come again, and receive you unto
Myself; that where I am, there you may be
also. And whither I go you know, and the
way you know.

Thomas said unto Him,
Lord, we know not whither You go;
and how can we know the way?

Jesus said unto him,
I am the way, the truth, and the life:
no man comes unto the Father,
but by Me" (Jn. 14:1-6).

"Peace I leave with you,
My peace I give unto you:
not as the world gives, give I unto you.
Let not your heart be troubled,
neither let it be afraid" (Jn. 14:27).

I intended to continue but she was too eager to leave, remembering some appointment and so forth. I wanted to move on with Psalm 19 and endeavor to show her some more of the glorious excellence of God's Word, and not only that, but hopefully try to introduce her and her husband to the wonderful God who has given us this thrilling revelation of Himself and of His wondrous works. Scripture is not a shrewd guess at truth; "Thy word is truth" (Jn. 17:17). It is the very consummate excellence of the Word of God that makes us stand still and worship Him with joy-filled adoration.

George Washington Carver, the genius has been called the world's greatest biochemist. By discovering hundreds of valuable uses for the peanut and sweet potato, he revolutionized Southern agriculture and rose to such prominence that *Thomas A. Edison* offered him a position at a salary running into six figures.

In 1921 Dr. Carver was invited to testify before the Senate Ways and Means Committee on the possibilities of the peanut. Given ten minutes to speak, he so enthralled the committee that the chairman said, "Go ahead, brother. Your time is unlimited." Carver talked for one hour and forty-five minutes, long past time for adjournment. At the conclusion of his address the chairman asked, "Dr. Carver, how did you learn all these things?" Carver replied, "From an old book." "What book?" the Senator inquired. Then came the great man's significant answer: "The Bible."

"Does the Bible tell about peanuts?" the surprised Senator queried. "No, sir," Dr. Carver replied, "but it tells about the God who made the peanut. I asked Him to show me what to do with the peanut, and He did."

"O Lord our Lord, how excellent is Thy name in all the earth!" (Ps. 8:9).